One plus One plus One

and 84 Other Wedding Sermons

Rev. Gary W. Fehring

CSS Publishing Company, Inc.
Lima, Ohio

ONE PLUS ONE PLUS ONE

FIRST EDITION
Copyright © 2013
by CSS Publishing Co., Inc.

Published by CSS Publishing Company, Inc., Lima, Ohio 45807. All rights reserved. No part of this publication may be reproduced in any manner whatsoever without the prior permission of the publisher, except in the case of brief quotations embodied in critical articles and reviews. Inquiries should be addressed to: CSS Publishing Company, Inc., Permissions Department, 5450 N. Dixie Highway, Lima, Ohio 45807.

Unless otherwise marked, scripture quotations are from the New Revised Standard Version of the Bible. Copyright 1989 by the Division of Christian Education of the National Council of the Churches of Christ in the USA, Nashville, Thomas Nelson Publishers © 1989. Used by permission. All rights reserved.

Some scripture quotations marked GNB or TEV are from the Good News Bible in Today's English Version. Copyright © American Bible Society 1966, 1971, 1976. Used by permission.

Some scripture quotations are marked Revised English Bible © Oxford University Press and Cambridge University Press 1989. Used by permission.

Some scripture quotations marked NIV are taken from the Holy Bible, New International Version. Copyright © 1973, 1978, 1984 International Bible Society. Used by permission of Zondervan Bible Publishers. All rights reserved.

Some scripture quotations marked (CEV) are taken from The Contemporary English Version with Apocrypha, Nashville, Tennessee, Thomas Nelson, 1997, © 1995 by the American Bible Society. Used by permission. All rights reserved.

Library of Congress Cataloging-in-Publication Data

Fehring, Gary W.
   One plus One plus One and 84 Other Wedding Sermons / Rev. Gary W. Fehring. -- FIRST EDITION.
      pages cm
   ISBN 0-7880-2698-4 (alk. paper)
   1. Wedding sermons. I. Title.

BV4278.F44 2013
252'.1--dc23

2012046839

For more information about CSS Publishing Company resources, visit our website at www.csspub.com, email us at csr@csspub.com, or call (800) 241-4056.

ISBN-13: 978-0-7880-2689-0
ISBN-10: 0-7880-2698-4   PRINTED IN USA

This collection of wedding homilies is dedicated to my wife Mary, for her encouragement during its preparation and throughout all the years of my parish ministry. Everything I have learned about marriage I have learned in companionship with her. Along with God's Word, Mary has been my best teacher about what marriage is and how good marriage can be.

Preface

In preparing for a marriage, it was my practice to have the couple choose the scriptures to be read at the ceremony. Because many themes of life converge in marriage and because the Bible speaks to all these themes, I encouraged couples to not simply pick scriptures that deal directly with the subject of marriage, but to explore such biblical themes as love, kindness, commitment, companionship, the goodness of life, the goodness of God's creation, joy, praise, faith, faithfulness to God, and faithfulness to others. The variety of their choices led to a variety of sermons.

Most of these homilies are fairly general and could be applied to many couples. A few relate more specifically to something about that particular couple. The homily, "To Heal as Jesus Did," was used at the wedding of two physical therapists, a situation not likely to occur with any frequency. "Go Fish" was done for a couple whose recreation was fishing. "The Frontier" was given at an outdoor wedding where the wedding party was dressed in western gear. For a couple in which the groom was a truck engine mechanic, "Tuning Up a Marriage" seemed appropriate.

All or nearly all of these homilies were written within the past ten years. I have tried to remove any references that would date them to a certain time or tie them to a specific location. I hope you enjoy reading them as much as I did preparing them.

Please remember that each of these homilies can be adapted to your church, the bride and groom, and the current situation.

Gary W. Fehring

* denotes the names of the bride and groom

Table of Contents

Sermon for a Small Wedding................................ 13
Genesis 2:18

Wedding Plans.. 15
Genesis 2-4

Ants and Earthworms (Outdoor Wedding).................. 17
Genesis 2:18-24; Ecclesiastes 4:9-12

Someone Like Me... 19
Genesis 2:18-24

Taken for Granted.. 21
Genesis 2:18-24

Good Fruit.. 24
Genesis 2:18-24; Luke 6:43-45

Gardening Chores... 26
Genesis 2:18-24

Learning About Marriage..................................... 28
Genesis 2:18-24; Ephesians 5:21-33;
1 Corinthians 13:4-7; John 15:12-16

Danger Ahead... 31
Genesis 2:18-24

Beginning Is the Easy Part.................................... 33
Genesis 2:18-24; Matthew 28:20

Discoveries.. 35
Genesis 2:18-24

Marriage Doesn't Add Up..................................... 37
Genesis 2:18-24; 1 Corinthians 13:4-7

God's Blessing.. 40
Numbers 6:24-26

Finding Happiness.. 42
Ruth 1:1-18

Where You Go.. 44
Ruth 1:16-17

Where You Go, I Will Go..................................... 46
Ruth 1:16-17

Being Polite... 48
Ruth 1:16-17

Goodness: Old and New. 50
Psalm 128; Genesis 2:24

God Cares. 52
Psalm 23

Lasting Happiness. 54
Psalm 128

God Loves Families. 56
Psalm 128

Simple Things. 58
Proverbs 21:21; 1 Corinthians 13:4-7; Ephesians 4:2-3

One Plus One Plus One. 60
Ecclesiastes 4:9-12

Joined Together. 62
Matthew 19:3-6; 1 Corinthians 13

Good Advice. 64
Matthew 5:1-16

The Garden Is Gone. 66
Mark 10:5-9

Something New or Something Old (Christmas Wedding). 68
Luke 2:1-20

Home for Christmas (Holiday Wedding) 70
Luke 15:11-24

Counting Costs. 72
Luke 10:30-35

Don't Worry. 74
Luke 12:22-31

New Beginnings. 77
Luke 7:11-17

Ordinary Things (Christmas Wedding). 79
Luke 2:8-12

I Have Called You Friends. 81
John 15:15

Love. 84
John 3:16, 13:34, 13:35, 15:13, 21:17; 1 Corinthians 13:13;
1 John 4:19; Ephesians 5:25; Song of Solomon 4:10

To Heal as Jesus Did (Two Physical Therapists' Wedding). 86
John 5:1-9; Psalm 100; Colossians 3:12-17; John 15:9-17

Love: Commanded and Encouraged. . . . . *John 15:12*	88
Marriage Advice. . . . . *John 15:9-16*	90
Jesus Is With You. . . . . *John 6:1-14*	93
Miracles in Marriage. . . . . *John 2:1-11*	95
Connections. . . . . *John 15:1-17*	97
Abiding in Love. . . . . *John 15:9-13; John 13:34*	99
Love in the Afternoon. . . . . *John 15:12-16*	101
A Successful Marriage. . . . . *Romans 12:1-21*	103
Be Transformed. . . . . *Romans 12:1-18*	105
What Marriage Is. . . . . *Romans 12; Philippians 4:8-9*	107
Without Love I Am Nothing. . . . . *1 Corinthians 13*	110
The Greater Gift. . . . . *1 Corinthians 12:31—13:8; 1 John 3:18-24*	113
Registered With God. . . . . *1 Corinthians 13; 1 John 4:7-12*	115
God Is Love (Apple Orchard Wedding). . . . . *1 Corinthians 13; 1 John 4:16*	117
Get Ready to Fight. . . . . *1 Corinthians 16:13-14*	119
Real Love and Real Life. . . . . *1 Corinthians 13; Romans 12:9-18*	121
Love or Nothing. . . . . *1 Corinthians 13*	124
The Frontier (Cowboy Wedding). . . . . *1 Corinthians 13:4-13; 1 John 4:14-21*	126
The Garden of Eden (Outdoor Wedding). . . . . *1 Corinthians 13:1-7*	128

Marvelous Words for Marriage.......................... 130
1 Corinthians 13; Philippians 4:4-9

Love: Before and After................................. 132
1 Corinthians 13

Perfect Love.. 134
1 Corinthians 13

The Look of Love...................................... 136
1 Corinthians 13

Marriage Is Giving.................................... 138
2 Corinthians 8:5

Heart Work and Head Work.............................. 140
Galatians 5:22-23a; Romans 12:2

The Chicken or the Egg................................ 142
Ephesians 5:21-33

Unromantic Love....................................... 144
Ephesians 5:21-33

Out of Respect for Christ............................. 146
Ephesians 5:21-33

Mutuality in Marriage................................. 148
Ephesians 5:21-33

Good Lessons for Life's Bad Days...................... 150
Philippians 1:3-11; Matthew 5:38-48

Wedding Gifts and Their Care.......................... 152
Philippians 2:1-11

Tuning Up a Marriage.................................. 154
Philippians 2:1-11

The Mind of Christ.................................... 156
Philippians 2:5-8; Matthew 16:24-26

Rejoice... 158
Philippians 4:4-9

Marriage Is Like a Gunny Sack......................... 161
Philippians 4:4-9

Go Fish... 163
Colossians 3:12-14

Wedding Dress... 165
Colossians 3:14

People of God... 168
Colossians 3:12-17; 1 Corinthians 13

Listening to God... 171
Colossians 3:12-14

Children of God (Two Successful People).................... 173
Colossians 3:12-17

So Much to See (Outdoor Wedding).......................... 175
2 Thessalonians 3:5

Sculpting a Marriage.. 177
1 Timothy 6:17-19

God's Good Gifts.. 179
James 1:17-18

Relationships: A Scientific Study........................... 181
James 3:2-12; Matthew 6:25-34;
Genesis 2:18-24; 1 Corinthians 12:31—13:13

Instructions.. 184
1 Peter 3:1-11; 1 Corinthians 13:1-8, 13

Sacrificial Love.. 186
1 John 4:7-19

Important Things.. 188
1 John 4:7-21

Knowing God.. 191
1 John 4:7-12

Love Each Other.. 193
1 John 4:7-21

Beautiful Words.. 195
1 John 4:7-21

Scriptural Index.. 197

Sermon for a Small Wedding
Genesis 2:18

This bride and groom* asked to have a small wedding. I assume, although they were too polite to come right out and request it, that also means a small wedding sermon.

As far as sermons are concerned, small is relative. I don't mean to scare you, but for Christians in places like India or Africa a "small" sermon couldn't be preached in less than an hour. On the opposite side, there are folks in this country, maybe some here today, who would only qualify a sermon as "small" if it was made up of two words or less. This wedding sermon falls in between those extremes. It isn't going to last an hour, but it is going to have more than two words. It is going to have three. I am not saying that it is only going to be three words long. What I am saying is that this "small" sermon is going to be about three words, three words that have a lot to say about marriage. Those three words come to us straight out of the word of God. Those words are companionship, love, and faith.

The Bible understands marriage as God's most profound answer to human loneliness. "It is not good that the man should be alone" (Genesis 2:18) is a statement by our Creator, and a truth of the human heart. Life alone is not only more difficult. The loneliness itself can be the greatest difficulty. Marriage is God's "companionship" answer to the loneliness and the difficulties of an alone life. Companionship is meant, in its sharing, to lighten the human load and to lighten the human heart.

Husbands and wives need to be coworkers and share the tasks of family living. Since the beginning that has been a part of the companionship of married life. But real marriage companionship must be more than just a division of labor. That might lighten the load, but it doesn't lighten the heart. For the companionship of marriage to lighten the heart, it must have love. Love, given from the heart for the purpose of lightening the heart of another, is what companionship is all about in our marriages and our families.

When husbands and wives care enough for each other and for their marriage to continue year after year, lightening each other's loads by how they share, and lightening each other's hearts by how they love, their marriage achieves its God-intended purpose as his companionship answer to aloneness and loneliness. That is what these two people* want their marriage to be for each other. That is what all of us here want your marriage to be for the two of you. That is what God wants your marriage to be for you both, a companionship filled with love and sharing.

That brings us to the third word of this three-word sermon. The word is faith. God wants your marriage to be for you every good thing he created marriage to be, to lighten your loads and to lighten your hearts. By your willingness to keep your life together open to God, open to his presence, open to his word, and open to his spirit-renewing gifts, you provide a resource for your marriage that has the ability to nourish and refresh its love and encourage and expand its companionship. Faith makes good things happen for a lifetime of companionship. May your faith provide access for you into the goodness God wants you to have in all the years of your life together.

I have done my best to keep this sermon small enough to meet your expectations. Faith assures us that God will do his best to give your marriage gifts that will be big enough to exceed your expectations. Love for each other that will continue to grow stronger. Companionship with each other that will continue to grow deeper.

In Jesus' name, Amen.

Wedding Plans
Genesis 2-4

The Adam and Eve story in Genesis 2-4 is one of the great stories, not only in the Bible but in all of human literature. Its imagery and poetry make it a wonderful story to read and ponder. There is the beauty of the garden, the loneliness of Adam, the attentive care of God, the parade of the animals, the creation of Eve, and the magic of that first face-to-face meeting of the couple. From that good beginning the story descends into disobedience and disaster: the tree, the serpent, the shame, the judgment, the loss of goodness, and the melancholy account of Cain and Abel. In the end, the statement made by this timeless story is a tragic one. Carelessness and disobedience brings ruin to what had been so good and so perfect.

There are two things in the Adam and Eve story that came to mind as I was reading it and thinking about the two of you, today's Adam and Eve. First, Adam and Eve never had to plan their wedding. They didn't send invitations, rent a hall for the reception, choose attendants, pick out dresses and tuxedos, select music, print up a bulletin, or wonder how long the pastor's sermon was going to be.

Adam and Eve never had to plan their wedding, but these two people* have. I would guess that our groom* would probably have been happy with an Adam and Eve wedding; just a few leaves, a kiss, and the blessing of God. Our bride* is the planner. She* has cared a lot about today, what will happen, and how things will look and sound. I have participated in a lot of weddings and I have been impressed with the attentiveness in which our bride* has planned today's event.

She wanted to make a statement. That's what planning does. Planning brings all the different things in a wedding together to make a statement, a statement about how special this day is, how beautiful this relationship is, and how much goodness is being celebrated and honored here today. How this day is seen and remembered is important. A lot of planning and work has been done to make today the best it can be.

The second thing that came to mind from the Adam and Eve story is how sadly it ends. Its final statement is about a goodness that has been lost. As important as it is to plan a wedding, it is even more important to plan a life together, to plan what that life should be so that not only the wedding day, but the whole of married life, makes a statement about specialness, beauty, and goodness.

Adam and Eve could have used a little planning in their life together. The first thing they should have planned was to build a fence around that tree. Instead, they just let things happen. I encourage the two of you* to make some good plans about your life together, not just house plans, or family plans, or money plans. Plan how you are going to use your love. Plan how you are going to use your faithfulness. Plan how you are going to use your care for each other. Plan how you are going to use your faith in God. Plan how you are going to use your living as God's people. As you plan, pray. As you pray, plan. Plan how all those things can fit together so that the goodness and beauty of today keeps going, alive and fresh, through all the days, months, and years ahead.

A lot of work has gone into this wedding. Work as hard — even harder — for your marriage. Plan and work so that the whole of your life together makes the statement you want it to make, not of God's goodness lost, but of God's goodness treasured and God's goodness shared.

Amen.

Ants and Earthworms
(Outdoor Wedding)
Genesis 2:18-24; Ecclesiastes 4:9-12

The God whose word we read in the Bible, and who opens himself for our inspection in Jesus Christ, is not a god of shapeless spirits and feathery kingdoms. God is God of soil and air, sun and grass, birds and flowers, grasshoppers, ants and earthworms. God is God of the germinating seed and the falling leaf. God is God of the angry storm and the caressing breeze, morning dew, noontime warmth, evening shadows, and the darkness of the night.

God is God of people, all people, all people in all the circumstances of their living. God is God of men and women, young lovers and lifelong companions. God is God of human skin in all its colors and of human hearts in all their passions.

God is God of lips meeting in a kiss, and God of fists clenched in battle. God is God of the words that give us comfort and of the words that give us pain. God is God of promises and patience and faithfulness and forgiveness. God is God of our new beginnings growing as they sometimes do, in the midst of life's sad, but necessary endings.

God is God of singleness, and God is God of marriage. There is no part of marriage that is beyond the rule, and beyond the goodness, of our Creator God. God's artistry is present everywhere in marriage, in the delight of its garden-kissed sexuality and in the joined hearts and hands that give marriage the life-affirming richness of its mutual support and care. God's creative touch can be felt everywhere in marriage bringing delight, strength, health and healing, building sacrificial commitment, weaving unity, enabling forgiveness, rewarding faithfulness, applauding loyalty, undergirding joy, and drying tears.

God makes possible the best of marriage. That, alone, is reason enough for husbands and wives to give God everything we are in worship, and everything we do in gratitude. God makes possible the best of marriage. In a world where love is advertised as beginning and ending only with the self, God shows what love is really like when we love this other who is ours in marriage. The army once said that it can make us the best we can be. That may be true of soldiers but not of husbands and not of wives. In marriage, God makes us the best we can be. For that we seek God's work within us, and God's work between us. Before God we join our hands in prayer and to God we turn our faces in hope and trust.

The two of you,* God is God of the world you live in, God is God of you, and God is God of your marriage. Wherever you may be in this world, walk with God. In those times when each of you may be alone, remember that even alone God is walking with you. Walk with him. As the couple God has made you, two people now one, walk with God. Seek God's blessing. Accept God's help. Give God your thanks for all the good things, all the best of things, God makes possible for the two of you in all your years of being together.

Amen.

Someone Like Me
Genesis 2:18-24

"Here is someone like me!" (Genesis 2:23 CEV). That's what Adam said when he first saw his wife-to-be, Eve. "Someone like me." The animals alone didn't do it for Adam. It was nice to have them around. It was kind of fun to give them names, but they didn't provide Adam the kind of companionship he needed. Even in their company Adam still felt lonely. Within the astonishing variety of animals God had created, there was not a single creature that was like him. God's response was to create Eve, the first woman. When God brought Eve to him, Adam knew at once that she was a whole different piece of work. "Here, at last," he said, "is someone like me!" Beneath the quiet dignity of biblical poetry, what Adam was really feeling and saying was more like, "Yahoo! God hit a home run this time! *This* is what I have been waiting for!"

Marriage hasn't changed at all. In all the thousands of years since the story of Adam and Eve was first shared among the people of God, at the heart of marriage is that wonderful feeling of, "Here at last is someone like me," or "Yahoo! This person, this relationship, is what I have been waiting for!"

The poetry, the joy, the unequaled delight of marriage is a gift from God. In God's kind and generous intent marriage adds a richness to human living that can be found nowhere else in life. "Here at last! This is what I have been waiting for!" These are God-pleasing expressions born in the hearts and souls of a man and a woman as they discover each other as partners for marriage. God surely finds joy when we express our enjoyment of his gift of marriage.

God puts the poetry in marriage. We human beings have a way of taking the poetry out. That's the sad truth. Taking the poetry out of marriage began with Adam and Eve in their world, and it continues with you and me in our world. Marriage is analyzed, dissected, studied, programmed, and twisted this way and that. We turn life together into a contest with winners and losers. There is no end to the joy-destroying effects people inflict upon the marriage relationship.

In so many ways we are so much more advanced than Adam and Eve. We know so much more about marriage than they did, except how to enjoy it, and how to make that enjoyment last for a lifetime. John and Julie*, God has given you to each other as surely as he gave Eve to Adam. Always remember that moment when Adam's words whispered in your own hearts. It was when you looked into each other's eyes and knew, "Here is someone like me."

Always remember that moment. Remember it because that moment was a God moment. The same God who gave that moment to Adam in the book of Genesis, gave it to each of you, "At last, this person, this relationship, is what I have been waiting for." God gave you your marriage. Today, as you receive his gift of marriage, give it back to him. Give your marriage back to God. It is so much safer in his hands than it will ever be in yours. Each day of your lifetime together, let God give your marriage back to you filled, as only God can fill it, with wonderful moments of poetry and delightful moments of joy.

Amen.

Taken for Granted
Genesis 2:18-24

From time to time there arises in every relationship the feeling of being taken for granted and not being appreciated for what we do. I suspect our bride* has felt that way when our groom* expected her to be really excited about spending an evening with him watching the six *Three Stooges* movies he rented. I suspect our groom* has felt he was being taken for granted when our bride* left him waiting in the car for what seemed like several hours while she went in to her girlfriend's house, for just a minute, to drop off her guest list for the bridal shower.

An important part of married living is expressing appreciation to each other. One way husbands and wives show how deeply they care for their partner is by taking the time to reassure them they are aware of, and grateful for, everything they do. John and Julie*, remember to build times of showing your appreciation into your life together.

But there is also something to be said for taking each other for granted. You can see that in our scripture lesson from Genesis 2. You know the story. God creates Adam and gives him a wonderful garden world in which to live. To make the happiness of this garden world complete he gives Adam and Eve to each other for a lifetime of companionship. Everything is perfect. There is food to eat. There are flowers to smell, sunsets to enjoy, a bright sun to warm the day, and stars and a moon to give a special brightness to the night. The animals Adam has named enjoy a friendship in a time and place when all creation was one and everything was good.

That's the way it was for Adam and Eve, and God was responsible for it all. All that goodness was God's gift to the two of them. What did God expect in return? Did God expect Adam and Eve to get down on their knees once or a dozen times a day to express their thanks? No. God looked for nothing for himself. God expected only that Adam and Eve would tend and care for the goodness of his garden world.

God allowed Adam and Eve to take him, and all he did for them, for granted. That was part of the gift. God wanted them to accept his gift as given and to show appreciation for it not in words and deeds toward him, but in words and deeds toward each other and toward the world around them, so that everywhere and in everything the goodness of God's gifts would grow and prosper. Giving thanks to God is not something Adam and Eve, or you and me, are expected to do. It is something they, and we, want to do. It is not a duty. It is a joy.

No one likes to be taken for granted. Sometimes we feel hurt when we think we are. However, husbands and wives can give each other the gift of allowing the other to take them for granted. That is a marvelous gift. It sets a person free from the continual worry of having to prove how much they appreciate their partner. Because you don't always expect your partner to show their gratitude to you for who you are and what you do; when words and deeds of appreciation do come, they come from the other person's heart, freely given and all the more marvelous. Taking each other for granted is a way of saying, "I trust you. I believe you care for me and appreciate me, even when you don't express it."

Taking each other for granted enables married couples to take their attention off the responsibility of always having to show their appreciation to each other and give that attention to working together as husband and wife. Their attention is now for tending and caring for home and family, congregation and community, working as a team to maintain the goodness of the gifts God gives to them and to his world.

John and Julie*, one of your wedding gifts can be the gift you give to each other. The gift of taking each other for granted. Don't abuse that gift by *never* showing your appreciation. I am sure no single day went without Adam and Eve saying "Thank you" to God for who God was and what God was doing for them. Let it be the same for you in the appreciation you show to God and to each other. Don't do it because that is what is expected. Do it because your hearts can't help themselves. The gratitude just comes out.

Don't abuse the gift of being able to take each other for granted. Celebrate that gift as partners, certain of the love and trust you have in and for each other. Certain of that, give your attention to the marvelous things you can do together for God and for God's world as husband and wife. In many ways, that's the best thanks you can show, to God, and to each other.

Amen.

Good Fruit
Genesis 2:18-24; Luke 6:43-45

"No good tree bears bad fruit" (Luke 6:43). That is what Jesus says in Luke's gospel, "No good tree bears bad fruit." "Every good tree bears good fruit" (Matthew 7:17). That is how Jesus says it in Matthew's gospel, "Every good tree bears good fruit."

Does that mean that good people have good marriages? It would be wonderful if that were always true. What is true is that husbands and wives who put good things into their life together have good marriages. The goodness of marriage depends on the good things put into it. If husbands and wives put good things like love, care, sensitivity, honesty, humility, encouragement, and compassion into their marriage, they will receive good things from their marriage. Not only will they receive good things from their marriage, their children will, and their families, friends, and neighbors will as well. A good marriage produces good things for everyone.

A good marriage produces good fruit. In Genesis 1 we are told that marriage is a part of the goodness of God's creation. "God saw everything that he had made, and indeed, it was very good" (Genesis 1:31). Marriage is not only a good thing. Marriage is a *very* good thing.

In Genesis 2 we are told that the goodness of marriage is all about companionship. The Lord God said, "It is not good that the man should be alone" (Genesis 2:18). God created marriage as a good thing. The companionship of marriage is meant to add goodness to human living.

If the Bible ended with Genesis 2, every marriage would be a good marriage, giving every married person the God-intended goodness of companionship. Unfortunately, there is a third chapter in the book of Genesis. Humankind did not treat God's good gifts, like marriage, with the goodness they deserve. Because of things like greed, pride, and selfishness, people have treated God's good gifts badly. People do that to many things. People do that to marriage. When people put bad things into their marriages, companionship is damaged. When companionship is damaged, the goodness of marriage is damaged. We see that happen in the Bible. We see that happen in the world.

God's good gifts deserve better from us. God's good gift of marriage certainly does. John and Julie*, the goodness of your marriage deserves the best you can put into it. That is going to take real commitment from both of you. There is going to be work for you to do individually, and work for you to do together. The work is worth doing. Your marriage is a gift God is giving you. The goodness of this gift is worth every good thing the two of you put into it.

"No good tree bears bad fruit, nor again does a bad tree bear good fruit" (Luke 6:43). If we apply these words of Jesus to marriage, we can say that nothing good is going to come from a bad marriage. That's not something we have to worry about, is it? This marriage is a good marriage. You knew that when you both said yes to your life together in marriage and you have the ring to prove it. You know that now with a new yes to each other and new rings for each other. This is a good marriage and good things are going to come from it, like good fruit from a good tree.

John and Julie*, always remember what you know today. Your marriage is a good marriage. Let the good things happen in the life you have begun to share together. Give goodness to each other. Find goodness in each other. A good marriage produces good things. Everyone here today, everyone you are going to meet in your journey together through life, is going to be glad to see those good things happen.

Amen.

Gardening Chores
Genesis 2:18-24

In that marvelous story in Genesis 2, we are told that God placed Adam in a garden to "till it and keep it" (Genesis 2:15). Within the great wisdom of the world, the complex philosophical, theological, and political answers about the place and purpose of human life, the biblical answer is embarrassingly simple. We are to live in the garden, in God's creation, to till it and keep it. You and I live in God's creation. That is our place. While we live here we are to tend the world's God-given goodness and take care of its God-given life. That is our purpose.

Our purpose is not to get rich from the world in which we live. God has placed us on this garden planet to enjoy and encourage the richness of the life around us, a shared richness with the air, water, soil, animals, and our neighbors. We are not to stand apart from creation, as though we are somehow superior and can do whatever we please. We are to live in creation as its caretakers and not its lords and masters. We are to look after, nourish, and support the life around us: wife, husband, children, neighborhood, nation, and world. We are all together as God's creation. We are all together sustained by God's divine presence.

"The Lord God took the man and put him in the Garden of Eden to till it and keep it" (Genesis 2:15). As the Genesis story continues, we learn that caring for the garden is lonely work. That was true for Adam and is also true for us. The goodness of God's garden can become overgrown with Satan's tangled underbrush. We want things to be better than they are. Trying to make that happen by ourselves can be so frustrating. We feel so alone.

That is why God created companionship. God's words in the Genesis story are "it is not good that the man should be alone; I will make him a helper as his partner" (Genesis 2:18). God created people as companions; to share the work, to encourage and support each other, to laugh together in good times, to cry together in bad times, to delight together when the garden blossoms with goodness, and to labor together against those things that threaten to rob the garden of any precious parcel of its goodness.

John and Julie*, God has placed you within his creation to tend it and to care for it. He has given you to each other to be companions, to live together enjoying all the goodness God is giving you, and to work together to keep that goodness happening for each other and the world around you. God doesn't care how much money you make. God doesn't care how nice your home may be. God doesn't care about the amount of stuff you may own. God doesn't care about where your jobs might rank on the status scale. God has given you to each other as companions, to live together in his name and as his children. God expects of the two of you what he expected of Adam and Eve; that you will be faithful in doing the work he created you to do to look after his world and, as best you can, help goodness to happen everywhere, for everyone, in everything.

Amen.

Learning About Marriage
Genesis 2:18-24; Ephesians 5:21-33;
1 Corinthians 13:4-7; John 15:12-16

How do we learn about marriage and what marriage is to be like? One way is to read books on the subject. There are many excellent books about marriage. Perhaps too many. I am afraid that couples who decide to read them all would end up spending more time with the librarian than with each other.

Another way to learn about marriage would be to read articles about it. It seems as though all magazines have them; *People*, *Us*, *Seventeen*, *Women's Day*, *Psychology Today*, *The Farm Journal*, and possibly even *Mechanics Illustrated* and *Field and Stream*. I imagine most of the magazine articles are helpful, but I am not sure it is fair to your mail carrier to subscribe to them all.

We can also learn about marriage from listening to other people. Usually the advice we get ranges from Henny Youngman jokes, "Take my wife... please," to a neighbor's ramblings that often begin, "Me and the Mrs..."

There is another, quite different, way of learning about what marriage is and what marriage is to be like. It is by looking at God. The Apostle Paul does that in the lesson from Ephesians that was read a few moments ago. In Christ we know what God is like. From the example of Christ we learn what marriage is to be like.

God cares about people. We see that in Christ's nurture and care for the people who are his church. We also witness God's care for people in the Genesis story. God is not only our Creator, but also our Caretaker. As God was deeply interested in Adam's well-being and gave him what he needed to bring goodness to his life, so is God deeply interested in the well-being of the whole human family, working to give us what we need to bring goodness to our lives.

Marriage is about people caring for people. Marriage is about one person being deeply interested in the well-being of another. Marriage is about one person working to give another person what they need to bring goodness to their life. We see in God, especially God in Christ, that caring for people is a way of life. Caring for people and caring for one another is a way of marriage too.

God chooses people. "You did not choose me but I chose you," says Jesus (John 15:16). God cares enough about people to know us, not just in a superficial, surface way. God knows us at the deepest level of our being. God knows our joys and sorrows. God knows our hopes and dreams. God knows us at our best, and God knows us at our worst. God cares enough to fully know us and knowing us, God chooses us to participate in the marvelous goodness of his salvation work.

Marriage, too, is about knowing and choosing. Marriage is about two people coming to know and continuing to know each other at the deepest level of their being, knowing the best and the worst about each other. Knowing the bad and the good, marriage is about two people choosing to share with each other a lifetime of goodness worked for and goodness given. God knows and chooses you and me. So, in marriage, husbands and wives know and choose each other.

"God is love" (1 John 4:8). When the Apostle Paul describes love in his letter to the Corinthians he is also, in a way, describing God. "[God] is patient; [God] is kind; [God] is not envious or boastful or arrogant or rude... [God] is not irritable or resentful, [God] does not rejoice in wrongdoing, but rejoices in the truth" (1 Corinthians 13:4-6).

As we relate to one another in marriage, the way we learn about the kind of person we ought to be is not only to read the words of the Apostle Paul as we have them in 1 Corinthians 13, but also to look at God and how God relates to us as Creator Father and companion Lord and Savior. The qualities of God that bring us such goodness in his relationship with us are qualities we are to develop in ourselves to bring that kind of goodness to our marriage.

God loves people. God loves us. In Jesus, God loves us enough to give his life for our well-being. Marriage is about that kind of love between persons, love that has no limits gives itself for the well-being of the other.

John and Julie*, during your engagement you have read, listened to, and learned a lot of good information about marriage. All of that will be to your advantage. There is much in the world, and even more in God, to help you understand what your marriage is to be like. Keep your eyes and your faith on God and his word as you continue to learn and build your life together in marriage.

Amen.

Danger Ahead
Genesis 2:18-24

I am always surprised when anyone who comes to talk to me about getting married actually goes through with it. I usually spend a great deal of time telling them about all the problems that can take place in a marriage. To the couples sitting in my office, I present marriage as being like a walk in the night along the edge of a cliff. At every moment there is the danger of taking a misstep and falling into the dark unknown.

I suspect I should be more positive. There are, after all, things in life that are more dangerous than marriage. Landing a jet fighter on the deck of an aircraft carrier in the middle of a hurricane is probably more dangerous than getting married. Although I can't be sure, I would think that earning a living by hunting poisonous snakes would have more, or at least as many, risks about it as being married.

There are things more dangerous than marriage. There are few things that are more pleasant. As we are told in Genesis 2, marriage is a gift of God given to add goodness to our lives. If things can go wrong and create a lot of pain and trouble in marriage, things can also go right and create a lot of joy and happiness in marriage.

God created marriage for human goodness, not for human misery. In spite of the problems we make in marriage, God is there to help us keep the goodness coming. When two people work, pray, and care to bring daily goodness to their life together, they can be sure that God adds his blessing to their efforts.

John and Julie*, look for, pray for, and work for the goodness of your marriage. That goodness is one of God's best gifts to your lives. Always know that it is not God's will for your marriage to be smashed to pieces on the rocks of the bad things that are happening in human living. Whenever you walk too close to that cliff edge and feel yourselves falling into the chasm of those painful problems plaguing marriages among us, look for God's strong hand to be there to catch you. Allow God to lift you out of danger. Allow God to bring you up and set you down on the solid ground of the goodness God has for your life together. God wants you both, and we want you both, to enjoy that goodness. God wants you both, and we want you both, to walk together in a lifetime of discovering everything God has for you in the goodness of your marriage.

Amen.

Beginning Is the Easy Part
Genesis 2:18-24; Matthew 28:20

Like so much of our own life histories, the Bible reminds us that beginnings are the easy part. For Adam and Eve, beginning their life together in the garden was the easy part. Staying in the garden was the hard part. In the end, it proved to be too hard. The story of Noah begins with Noah's family working happily together building the ark. By the end of the story it is brother against brother, and father against son. The story of the exodus from Egypt begins with Israel standing on the northern shore of the Red Sea singing songs of praise and victory. As their journey to the Promised Land continued, each hardship brought a chorus of complaints. Faith became idolatry and many of those who left Egypt died before setting foot in the new land God was giving them. David's story begins with his trust in God, and his victory over Goliath. Later David would put aside that trust and pursue his passion into adultery and murder. The story of Jesus begins in the joyful wonder of the manger and the worship of shepherds and kings. Later in the story the manger gives way to the cross. Instead of worshiping Jesus, the crowds were cursing him.

The beginning is the easy part. That is often true in the Bible. It is always true in marriage. As much of a hassle as planning and having a wedding can be for a marriage, it is the easy part. Today's divorce rate is clear evidence that the most difficult time for a marriage comes after the wedding day, in the days, weeks, months, and years of married life.

John and Julie*, as you begin your marriage, God is surrounding you with his love, his blessing, and his support. Know that your marriage will need God's love, blessing, and support, even more in the days to come. As you have invited God into your wedding today, continue to invite God into your married life. Let God help you make this good beginning lead into a story in which each chapter of your marriage will have its special happiness and goodness.

The Lord, who is here today, has promised to be with you at the beginning, the middle, and for the future of your life together as husband and wife. It's a promise Jesus will keep. It's a promise your marriage will always have and will always need.

Amen.

Discoveries
Genesis 2:18-24

Human beings have a natural ability to discover things. The wheel, fire, electricity, penicillin, radio waves, and french fries are just a few of humankind's amazing discoveries. The first discovery made by a human being was made by a man named Adam. God created Adam and placed him in a garden to tend and keep it. Adam's discovery was loneliness.

Adam had the best of life as God could give it. He had health, beauty, food in abundance, security, peace, and the surrounding presence of a loving, caring God. Everything in and around Adam was perfect. Everything in and around him was good. With all of that, Adam's first discovery was his own loneliness. Goodness is only truly good when it is shared. Even faith and trust in a wonderful God needs to make deep contact with another human being for its richness to fully blossom.

Adam discovered loneliness. Unlike discoveries such as the wheel and fire, which once made do not have to be remade, Adam's loneliness is a discovery every human being has had to make for themselves. Whatever the circumstances of our lives, in the midst of joys or sorrows, moments when life is almost ideal, moments when life borders on total disaster, in the living out of our lives we each make our own discovery of the reality of loneliness.

The God who was with Adam when Adam discovered his loneliness is with you and me when we discover ours. This God, who knows us better than we know ourselves, responds to our loneliness by saying, "[This] is not good" (Genesis 2:18). God answers our loneliness by opening our eyes to other people. That is the only cure for loneliness. To those who discover loneliness God gives the opportunity to discover other people to laugh with, cry with, work with, relax with, share our faith with, share our fears with, and share our hopes and dreams with.

As Adam discovered Eve, and with her, God's companionship answer to the loneliness he had found in himself, so John and Julie*, you have discovered each other. You have discovered in each other God's companionship answer to any loneliness you have found within yourselves. You are given a lifetime together to discover and rediscover how to offer your companionship as the God-given answer you each need for your lives to be truly good. That is what we all hope and pray for. That kind of goodness for your life together.

One of the intriguing aspects of married life is the ongoing process of husbands and wives discovering things about each other. A wife discovers that her shy, quiet husband snores so loudly the windows rattle. A husband discovers that the color of his wife's hair doesn't come from her DNA. It comes from her beautician. A wife discovers that her husband does not like zucchini. A husband discovers that zucchini is the only thing his wife can cook.

John and Julie*, you are pledging yourselves to a lifetime of discovering all sorts of things about each other. Use those discoveries as opportunities to express in new ways your love and your companionship.

Amen.

Marriage Doesn't Add Up
Genesis 2:18-24; 1 Corinthians 13:4-7

Some of my favorite films are the old black and white Charlie Chan detective movies. In old movies Charlie Chan's number one son was never quite able to keep up with his father in figuring out what was going on. Somewhere in the course of the story the bewildered young man would puzzle over the events taking place and utter this classic piece of dialogue, "Gee, Dad, that just doesn't add up."

In the film he wasn't talking about marriage, but he could have been. In many ways marriage is something that "doesn't add up." It is not just a matter of numbers, such as the Genesis arithmetic where two become one. What doesn't add up has to do with the whole lifetime process of living together as husband and wife.

Mathematics is perfect and precise. When we are good at it, we already know how the answer is going to come out before we begin to work through the problem. In mathematics, as I learned in school, there are no surprises. Two plus two is always four and the square root of nine is always three. In mathematics we have things in our control. If we do things right, the numbers we use perform beautifully. Because God is God of everything in heaven and on earth, God is God of mathematics. God has created mathematics so well it sort of runs without him. The solution to a problem of addition does not change because of God's involvement with it.

Marriage is nothing like arithmetic. Marriage is never perfect or precise. Because people are not perfect, the relationship between people has its imperfections. Marriage is made up of strengths and weaknesses, successes and failures. If anyone enters a marriage expecting things to move smoothly and perfectly, like a well-arranged equation, that person is going to be very disappointed.

John and Julie*, be willing to live with the imperfections in each other and with the imperfections in your marriage. Understand those imperfections, adjust to them, and work out your marriage around them. If things don't always add up as perfectly as you might want, be happy. You married a person, not the number six.

Unlike mathematics, marriage is full of surprises. What seemed to add up to four one day might add up to five the next. You can never be sure how things are going to work themselves out in your life together.

John and Julie*, don't be upset by the surprises taking place in your relationship. If you live in love and faithfulness to each other and work at keeping the vows you are making today, the surprises that come will not undermine your marriage but will instead enrich and enliven it. Nothing could be more boring than doing the same mathematical problem over and over again. Be thankful your marriage will not be like that.

Mathematics is a matter of controlling the numbers and the equations until you arrive at the solution. Marriage is not a matter of control. Marriage is a matter of love. Marriage is not a matter of manipulation, putting things exactly where you want them. Marriage is a matter of care, support, understanding, and encouragement. In marriage something very precious is destroyed when the people in the marriage try to control and manipulate each other, like numbers on a sheet of paper.

John and Julie*, remember the Apostle Paul's words in 1 Corinthians: "Love is patient; love is kind; love is not envious or boastful or arrogant or rude. It does not insist on its own way" (1 Corinthians 13:4-5). Paul is writing about how the two of you are to treat each other, as people you are given to love, not as numbers you want to use.

Maybe mathematics does not require God's involvement, but marriage certainly does. Marriage needs God's continuing power of renewal. Marriage needs the forgiveness that comes from God to be shared between people. Marriage needs God's gift of new beginnings. Marriage needs prayer. Marriage needs God's guidance. Marriage needs continual consideration of God's word, and what God's word teaches us about living as his children. Marriage requires the constant intervention of God so that it retains the goodness God created marriage to have. People don't usually pray for two plus two to equal four, but all the people here are praying that God's blessing and support will make John and Julie's* marriage a long and happy one.

John and Julie*, invite God's involvement in your life together. Accept God's gifts. Be open to God's guidance. In good times, share with each other all the good things God is giving you. In hard times, encourage each other with the comfort and support that is there for you in God's word and in God's love.

Marriage is something that doesn't always add up. John and Julie*, accept that and in love and faith and faithfulness, make the most of it. Live out the goodness of your marriage as the God who is making the two of you into one adds his presence to your life together.

Amen.

God's Blessing
Numbers 6:24-26

Of all the wedding presents you receive, I wonder which will be the best. If the two of you don't have anything better to do on your honeymoon, why not make a list of all your wedding presents and pick which gift is the best. I suppose you could choose the toaster, the slow cooker, or the set of dish towels for every day of the week. I'm sure these good people here are giving you some really nice gifts.

One of your wedding guests is giving you the best gift of all. That guest is God. The gift is God's blessing on your life together. That is something only God can give. When you add God's blessing to your list of wedding presents, your choice of which is the best gift is made for you. For usefulness and durability, in almost every way, no other gift comes close to God's gift of his blessing.

In a couple of weeks you will probably be putting a few of your wedding presents away to be used sometime in the future. You might put some of them away so well you will forget you have them. Be sure not to do that with God's blessing. Never forget you have it.

Let God's blessing direct you to seek the goodness God has for you, as a couple and as a family. Let God's blessing draw you together on those days when you feel yourselves pulling apart. If there are times when something precious in your marriage seems to be ending, let God's blessing open up wonderful new beginnings. All the hope you will ever need, all the happiness you will ever need, all the love for each other you will ever need is there for you in the blessing God is giving you today, the blessing God will continue to give you every day of your marriage.

Trust in God's blessing. Celebrate it. See it in each other's eyes. Feel it in each other's touch. Hear it in each other's voice. Let each experience of worship remind you of the blessing the two of you have received. Let God's word teach you more about what his blessing means and what his blessing does. Let God's blessing be included in your daily bread. Receive it with thanksgiving. Live it out with faith and faithfulness.

Now, John and Julie*, "The Lord bless you and keep you; the Lord make his face to shine upon you, and be gracious to you; the Lord lift up his countenance upon you, and give you peace" (Numbers 6:24-26).

Amen.

Finding Happiness
Ruth 1:1-18

The book of Ruth is about a person making one of the biggest sacrifices anyone can make — the sacrifice of one's self. "Where you go, I will go," Ruth says. "Your people shall be my people, and your God my God. Where you die, I will die — there will I be buried" (Ruth 1:16-17).

Ruth gives up her independence, her free choice, her self-reliance. Ruth allows her life to be dependent on the decisions and choices of someone else. Before you women here begin to call me names like macho pig, jerk, and accuse me of male prejudice, I need to remind you that Ruth did not give up her independence because of some guy. Ruth gave up her independence because of a woman, her mother-in-law, Naomi.

It was in the sacrifice of herself that Ruth found herself. Although from then on her life was not always easy, there was happiness in it, and there was a happy ending to it. "Not what I want but what you want" (Matthew 26:39). Those Ruth-like words are the words of our Lord Jesus as he gave up his life for his heavenly Father and for us. That sacrifice of himself led Jesus to the pain of the cross, and through that pain to the joy of resurrection. "He humbled himself and became obedient to the point of death — even death on a cross. Therefore God has highly exalted him and gave him the name that is above every name" (Philippians 2:8-9).

"For those who want to save their life will lose it, and those who lose their life for my sake will find it" (Matthew 16:25). Those words are also the words of Jesus. At this time in history, people seeking happiness have a real need to listen to what Jesus is saying. The trend today is to find happiness by holding onto ourselves, each of us living life our way. Sacrifice is measured not in a lifetime, but in minutes, minutes when we must give up doing what we want because we have to do what someone else wants. We begrudge every second.

You tell me if that is the way to happiness. I don't see it. It seems to me that Ruth had a better idea. None us will be following the example of Jesus, but all of us can follow the example of Ruth, especially in our marriages. Instead of fighting for happiness for ourselves, like Ruth we relax our grip on ourselves and seek our happiness in the company of another. It is in our dependence on God, and our interdependence on one another, that happiness has a way of finding us.

The happiness Ruth found in life she found not by looking out for herself, but by giving up herself. May it be that every married person finds the happiness they are seeking not by looking out for themselves in their marriages but giving themselves up in their marriages, "Not what I want, but what we want." Our groom and bride*, you know that God loves you. Find your happiness in your dependence on him. Our groom*, you know that your bride* loves you. Our bride*, you know that our groom* loves you. In that love, find your happiness by depending upon each other. "Not what I want, but what God wants. Not what I want, but what we want."

Amen.

Where You Go
Ruth 1:16-17

We live in a strange society. Because of constant movement, we often find ourselves surrounded by strangers. Old friends and family are often far away. Even our closest neighbors are people we don't even know. The people around us can be friendly enough. Still, living among friendly people is not the same as living among people who know you and care about you, people who have a stake in how your life is going, and people who really listen and who will always be there for you when you need them.

What is strange about our society is that instead of praising companionship and closeness, because the need for it is so desperate, our society seems bent on driving people apart. Competition, not companionship, is a way of life for us, not just on the field, the court, or the rink, but at the work place, the shopping center, the highway, and even in marriage. "Look out for yourself," we say. "Make yourself happy," we say. "You are the only one who really matters," we say.

These modern expressions are almost exactly the same as the 3,000-year-old words Naomi spoke to Ruth in the verse previous to those just read. Naomi was Ruth's mother-in-law. Early death was common in that time, and both Ruth and Naomi had lost all their loved ones. Naomi had been living in Ruth's country, but now she was going home. Ruth intended to go with her, even though it meant going to a country whose language she didn't know and whose religion and customs she did not share. Naomi knew how difficult that was going to be for Ruth so she told her not to follow but to return to her own home. "Look out for yourself, Ruth," Naomi was saying, "make yourself happy." Ruth didn't want to do that. Ruth treasured her relationship with Naomi. For Ruth it was in maintaining that relationship, not in looking out for herself, that she found meaning in life. Our scripture lesson gives us the words Ruth used to express the value of her relationship with Naomi. John and Julie* have included them in their wedding because Ruth's words express the value they are giving to their relationship with each other.

> Where you go, I will go; where you lodge, I will lodge; your people shall be my people, and your God my God. Where you die, I will die — there will I be buried.
> (Ruth 1:16-17)

John and Julie*, in a lonely world the two of you have come together as companions; to care and to be cared for, to listen and to be listened to, to understand and to be understood, to always be there with and for each other. Celebrate this relationship, as all of us are celebrating it with you today. Treasure this relationship for its goodness. In the days, weeks, months, and years to come, continue to celebrate, treasure, and find value for yourselves in your relationship as husband and wife. When our world seeks to drive the two of you apart, remember the words of Ruth and rededicate yourselves to life together. God is telling you, and all of us, how important relationships are. May they be as important to you, and us, as they are to God.
Amen.

Where You Go, I Will Go
Ruth 1:16-17

There is not much in the book of Ruth to make it memorable to us. It does tell an interesting enough story about the great-grandmother of King David, but there are no miracles in the story, no great acts of deliverance, and no mighty deeds of faith. Were it not for the one short passage in Ruth that has just been read, the story of Ruth would be as obscure as so many other interesting Bible stories, like the stories of Jephthah, Abemelech, or Ehud.

It is the simple statement of Ruth to her mother-in-law Naomi that makes the book of Ruth a treasure, not just to the church, but to the world. "Where you go, I will go" (Ruth 1:16) is a commitment to companionship. A pledge that, in a world of lonely people, each moving about on their own, there is one person willing to put aside going their own way to go the way of another human being.

That is truly a remarkable thing. It is surpassed in existence only by God himself, who chose, in Jesus, to no longer go his own way. In Jesus, God has become the companion of every single human being in creation. We know how difficult it was for Jesus to go where we go, even into death with us. Real companionship is sacrifice. It was that for Jesus. It was that for Ruth. It is that for every husband and every wife. In companionship we give up something of ourselves and replace it with something that is another's. Jesus took our sin. Ruth adopted Naomi's country. In marriage, a husband and a wife each give up the "I" of who they always were and replace it with the "we" of who they have forever become. That is both the cost and the joy of companionship.

The joy of Jesus' companionship with us is Jesus taking us with him into his heavenly Father's favor and his heavenly Father's house. The joy of Ruth's companionship brought her to the love of her life and her special place in the greatest story ever told: the story of God at work for our salvation. The greatest joy in any marriage happens at those moments when companionship is felt at the deepest places of the soul.

"Where you go, I will go." Ruth's commitment to companionship has become a treasure for us to read. John and Julie*, the commitment to companionship the two of you are making today is a delight for us to witness. May your mutual pledges of companionship make your life as beautiful among us as the story of Ruth is beautiful in the Bible.

Amen.

Being Polite
Ruth 1:16-17

As I sat at my desk pondering these great Bible passages included in John and Julie's* wedding, I thought about all the themes they contain: companionship, love, commitment. Like they do in the advertising business, I ran each of these themes up the old flagpole to see if I could get anyone in the bleachers to stand up and salute. Nothing. The crowd just yawned and ate their popcorn. Even the bugler complained. "Good stuff," he told me, "but it's all been said before." "Try being polite," he said, "and keep still." Then I thought, "That's it! That's what I'll do! I'll talk about being polite!"

We are not polite people anymore, not most of us. We are aggressive. We are wrapped up in ourselves. In our lives we are always pushing ahead, doing what we have to do. That's the way we are told to be. Being aggressive pays off. Being polite is old-fashioned. Even marriage is presented in aggressive terms. To us, a successful marriage is an alliance of two aggressive people who agree to push their way through life together.

Let me take a moment to speak for politeness. Being polite is more than having good table manners, using the right deodorant, or holding the door. Being polite is recognizing that other people really do exist and must be respected. Being polite is accepting the fact that life is not just about ourselves but about ourselves in relationship to others. Being polite is the willingness to be second sometimes so that another person can be first.

Being polite is what Ruth was in our scripture lesson. Ruth and her sister Orpah had accompanied their mother-in-law, Naomi, as Naomi began her journey back to Israel. At the border of Israel, Naomi wished Ruth and Orpah well and suggested that they return to their own people. It was the sensible thing to do, and Orpah did it. Ruth could have gone back to the people whose language she understood and whose customs she shared. Instead of doing what was best for herself, Ruth was willing to do what was best for Naomi. That was being polite, putting Naomi first. "Where you go, I will go; where you lodge, I will lodge; your people shall be my people, and your God my God" (Ruth 1:16). With those words Ruth stood back to allow Naomi to take the lead.

We are not even polite to God. We constantly tell God how we want things; "I want to be happy or healthy." "God, what would it hurt to make me rich?" "So, God, I told you what I want. Now it's time for you to do your stuff. Amen." It is a different prayer than the prayer Jesus prayed in the garden, "[Father] not what I want, but what you want" (Mark 14:36).

There is a place in marriage for being polite, for stepping back, and letting our partners take the lead, "Where you go, I will go." There is a place in marriage for being polite, for husbands and wives to disagree not on who is going to be first and get their way, but for husbands and wives to disagree on who gets the privilege, this time, of letting their partner go first. "Tell me where you want to go, and I will follow."

Being polite puts a leash on the aggressive nature we too often allow to run wild. We need to do that in our relationships with one another and our relationship with God. If there is any place we need to be polite, it is with God. With gentle grace we pray, "God, where you go, I will go. Not what I want, but what you want." As husbands and wives we pray, "God, where you go, we will go. Not what we want, but what you want."

John and Julie*, to your love and care for each other, to your commitment to each other, to all those things making you one today, add politeness. Add that gentle willingness to stand aside for God and for each other. Today, when you say your vows, whoever goes first doesn't matter. Let it be that way in your life together. Invite each other to go first, be always willing to follow, in good times and in bad, in sickness and in health, in joy and in sorrow, as long as you both shall live.

Amen.

Goodness: Old and New
Psalm 128; Genesis 2:24

The scripture lessons you have included in your wedding speak of both separation, a going apart, and unification, a coming together.

"Therefore a man leaves his father and his mother" (Genesis 2:24 NRSV). Here is the separation. A person goes away, moves apart, and leaves family behind.

When something is good, when our own lives in our own families have been filled with goodness, this separation, this moving apart, seems so unwise, so unnecessary. In Psalm 128 we read that family life, lived by faithful people, is blessed by God and filled with God-given goodness. Why would someone leave something that is not only good but also has the blessing of God?

Yet aware as we are of the goodness of family life, not one person here would say, "Don't go." There might still be time for both of you, our bride and groom*, to make a dash out the door, jump into a car, and go back home where you belong, but nobody here would want you to do that. As good as home can be, we know that home is not where the two of you belong. You belong together.

"Therefore a man leaves his father and his mother and clings to his wife" (Genesis 2:24). That is union, coming together. Two separate people uniting to become one, leaving everything of their separate lives behind, including home and family.

The reason for your leaving home and family is that, in your coming together as partners in marriage, God is creating a new goodness that each of you will share. This "new goodness" grows out of your love for each other as God's Spirit inspires you to love in all these beautiful ways. Love is described in the word of God: patient, kind, gentle, respectful, humble, self-sacrificing, forgiving, believing the best, hoping for the best, and working to create the best in life together. Loving each other the way Jesus loves you.

In this coming together, which today is all about, God creates a new goodness for each of you to share. It is a goodness experienced in your love for each other. It is a goodness experienced in your faithfulness to God. Through that love and that faithfulness God is creating for you a special goodness that is warm with his blessing.

Just so, a new family is born, your family, a family coming to be out of your "going apart" and, today, of your "coming together." A new family, living out new faithfulness, finding a new blessing and enjoying new goodness.

May God's rich blessing be so abundant in the goodness of this new family of yours that, in a couple dozen years, this sermon can be preached again, the question asked again of your own child. "How can you leave something so good as the family you have grown up in?"

The answer for your child will be the same answer as it is for you. Old goodness must be left behind so that God can create a new goodness. Old goodness must be left behind so that two of his children can live out a new faithfulness. Old goodness must be left behind so that a new family can experience God's new blessing.

Amen.

God Cares
Psalm 23

John and Julie*, you have chosen a marvelous scripture lesson to be included in your wedding. "The Lord is my shepherd," it begins, "I shall not want" (Psalm 23:1). These familiar words of God speak to us of his goodness, the love God has for people, and the care with which God looks after each of us as a shepherd looks after his sheep. The words of this wonderful Psalm tell us of God's readiness to help and support those who depend on him.

We need to know that. The two of you need to know that in your life together. As young as the two of you are, you already know that life in the world is not always easy. Things happen. Things never stop happening. Life can have problems. In choosing to be married, the two of you have chosen to face life's problems together. That is a wonderful thing to do. It is going to bring a real difference, making many of life's problems easier to handle.

Many of life's problems will be easier but not all of them. As husband and wife, you need to know that you can depend upon each other. You also need to know that you can depend upon God. There will be times when you can't find green pastures to lie down in. There will be times when still waters are stirred up by powerful storms. There will be times when the valleys you have to walk through will be frighteningly dark. In those times, especially, you need to know that God will be there for you. God is speaking to you in this Psalm. He is telling you that he is going to do just that. In your life together, when you need God, he will be there for you. Because your marriage has God's blessing, it also has his help.

John and Julie*, don't be afraid when problems come in to your life together. Accept God's invitation to bring those problems to him in prayer. Allow God to give you the help you need to get through them, no matter how impossible that might seem.

God has always been with each of you. God made that promise to you when you were baptized. From today onward, God will be with you as husband and wife. Whenever the cup of your married life seems to be running dry, trust in God that the time is coming when it will be filled to overflowing with God-given richness and blessing.

God is going with you as husband and wife, today, tomorrow, and all the days to come. Because that is true, "surely goodness and mercy shall follow [you] all the days of [your] life" (Psalm 23:6).

Amen.

Lasting Happiness
Psalm 128

In the Psalm John and Julie* have chosen to include in their wedding, we are told that those who put their trust in God will be happy. What do you suppose that means? It can't mean that people who trust in God will have nothing but joy in their lives, nothing but joy in their marriages, no troubles, no problems, no sorrow or grief, no pain or disappointment. The Psalmist knew what all of us know: bad things happen. Bad things happen, even to good people.

All of us want John and Julie* to live happy lives, and especially today, we want John and Julie* to have a happy marriage. God wants that too. Because the two of them are putting their trust in God; putting their lives, marriage, and family in God's hands; God promises to give them everything they need to have happy lives and a happy marriage.

God doesn't promise that John and Julie* will never have any problems or troubles in their lives or in their marriage. What God does promise is that no matter what troubles or problems this world might bring them, no matter how bad or difficult those troubles or problems might be, God will always be there for them. No matter what troubles or problems this world might bring in their lives, and in their life together, no matter how bad those troubles or problems might be, John and Julie* will never be without God's love, healing, forgiveness, strength, and encouragement. Should there be times in their lives and in their marriage when every door to goodness seems locked to them, God will be there with his power to open those doors and open new ways, new beginnings, into the goodness he has for them.

That is where happiness comes from. Real, lasting, sustaining happiness comes from knowing that nothing can take God's goodness away from our lives and nothing can take God's goodness away from our marriages. When we look for it, God will make sure we find it or are found by it.

John and Julie*, everyone here is hoping and praying that in your life together the two of you will be happy. We hope and pray that you will experience days, weeks, months, and years of happy, smiling, joyful times. On those days not like that, days when it is hard, even impossible, for you to smile, we hope and pray that God will provide you the deep, sustaining happiness that comes from knowing that, in spite of how bad things seem at the moment, God's goodness is still there with you and for you. We hope and pray that God's deep, sustaining happiness will enrich you, renew you, and carry you through all those experiences of life that are anything but good.

John and Julie*, God gives happiness to those who put their trust in him. Because you are doing that, may the happiness God gives be reflected in all the years of your lifetime together in marriage.

Amen.

God Loves Families
Psalm 128

God loves families. God loves families because God loves people, and God loves those things that make the people he loves happy. That's what families are about, making people happy. At least that is what God wants families to be about. God involves himself in family life in order to provide happiness to people.

God involves himself in family life by listening to our prayers. God listens to our prayers when we pray together as families. God listens to our prayers when we pray alone for our families. God listens to our prayers, giving to us the happiness of knowing that our families have him as our good and caring friend.

God involves himself in family life by assuring us of his love for us. God gives every family member the assurance that they are kept securely in his love. By being loved so well by God, each family member can happily give themselves in love for one another and happily give themselves in love to their brothers and sisters in the world.

God involves himself in family life by accepting each of us as we are. We don't have to prove a thing to God. God wants us to know that we are precious to him just as we are. Each of us being precious to God makes us precious to each other. We don't have to prove anything to each other in our families. There are two happy places where we are always accepted as we are. When we are with God. When we are within our families.

God involves himself in family life by sharing his guidance with us through the Holy Spirit. God does not just set down rules for family living. God supports and encourages us, gifting us through the Holy Spirit to love each other and to treat each other with kindness and patience, gentleness and trust. When families learn from God how to love each other the way God loves us, families experience a special kind of happiness.

God wants families to be happy. God involves himself in family life in order to provide happiness to all the people in that family. Our contributions toward family living are not always so clearly directed as God's. We sometimes say and do things that make members of our family unhappy. Sometimes we do that by accident. Sometimes we do that by intent.

John and Julie*, love your marriage and love your family as God does. You will never be able to love them as much as God does. You will never be able to provide your marriage and your family as many reasons for happiness as God does. But try. Take it as your daily task to make each other, and your children, happy as a family. Make good use of everything God is giving you and of everything you have to give to make happiness happen.

Amen.

Simple Things
Proverbs 21:21;
1 Corinthians 13:4-7; Ephesians 4:2-3

Reading our scripture lessons reminds us that in our relationship with God it is the simple things that matter most. Very few of us are like Noah, braving the ridicule of our neighbors by building an ark far from any lake or river. Very few of us are like Moses, leading a whole nation out of slavery. Very few of us are like David, walking out on the battlefield with only a slingshot to face the armor-clad, sword-swinging giant, Goliath.

Most of us will not be doing the kind of great things for God that will get us written up in books and made into movies. But we all talk to God in simple prayers. We all believe the simple truth that God loves us and keeps the promises he makes to us. All of us keep the simple values of loving God and loving our neighbors as the guiding principles of our lives.

Those are simple things. They may not always be easy to do, but they are simple enough that even a child can understand them. Those things, the simple things, are the things that matter most in our relationship with God.

Reading our scripture lessons also remind us that in our relationship with one another, it is the simple things that matter most. Every married person knows what our lessons teach us about simple things being the most important and that is certainly true in marriage. Very few of us are like Shakespeare, writing poetry of love that will be admired for a thousand years. Very few of us are like Donald Trump, buying our beloved diamonds as big as baseballs. Very few of us are like Pocahontas, throwing our own bodies between our beloved and the thrusting spear. Very few of us are expected to fill our married lives with moments that get our smiling faces on the cover of *People* magazine. But all of us are expected to be honest with our partner in marriage. All of us, husbands and wives, are expected to be kind to each other.

In marriage, patience with each other is among the most important things. So is trust and humility and so is respect and the willingness to go the extra mile. In marriage people ought not snap at each other or hold a grudge. Forgiveness and acceptance are important things in every marriage. Just as important is the desire to make your partner happy.

All those things mentioned and others like being tolerant and gentle, are simple things. They are the things that matter most in marriage. Those simple things are not always easy to do. I wish they were. The divorce rate in our country would be zero if they were easy to do. They may not be easy for all of us to always do in our marriages, but they are easy enough for all of us to understand. Understanding these simple things, it is up to each of us to live them out in our lives and in our marriages.

The two of you*, in whatever plans you make, in whatever direction your life together takes you, in whatever circumstance you find yourselves, never forget the simple things that matter most. Talk to God in prayer, accept God's love and believe his promises. Love God and love your neighbors. Toward each other be honest and kind, gentle and humble, trust each other, show respect for each other, and go the extra mile for each other. Be generous with your forgiveness and enthusiastic in your desire to make each other happy.

God wants you to know it is in those simple things that you will find real goodness in your life with him and goodness in your marriage to each other.

Amen.

One plus One plus One
Ecclesiastes 4:9-12

Let me tell you something about God that you may not know. God loves mathematics! That's unusual. Jesus has told us that God is Spirit. God doesn't have fingers. How does he count? Without a place to buy batteries for a calculator, how in heaven can God do multiplication and division? If I were God I would hate mathematics, but God doesn't. God loves it.

God loves to use mathematics. God looks at the number one, one Adam and one Eve, one bride* and one groom*. God looks at those pairs of ones and says to himself, "I am going to add those numbers together, one Adam plus one Eve, one bride* plus one groom*." When you and I add one and one together we often come up with two. As the writer of Ecclesiastes reminds us, two is an awfully good number. Two people together, one bride* and one groom* have all sorts of good things to give to each other, and all sorts of good things to share with each other.

When God adds one and one together they sometimes equal two but not always. Sometimes in God's mathematics one plus one equals one. In a little while, our bride* and our groom* are going to demonstrate that for us. They are going to add the flame of one candle to the flame of another candle. What they are going to end up with is not two flames, but one. One flame, plus one flame, equals one flame.

One bride* plus one groom* equals one brand new person. One I, plus one I, equals one we. One me, plus one me, equals one us. Sometimes we call this new person Julie*. Sometimes we call this new person John*. Sometimes we call this new person John and Julie*. But it isn't two people, not in God's mathematics it isn't. In God's math our bride* and our groom* are one person, with one heart, one hope, one life, one future, and one family.

The thing about one is that it is a very hard number to divide. You can't do it by using your fingers, unless you have a decimal point for a thumb. Jesus tells us that God means it to be that way. God doesn't want us to try dividing into two what he adds up as one. Every married person needs to remember that and not mess with God's math.

For God, one, plus one, can sometimes equal two. There are other times, times like today, when, one, plus one, equals one. There are other times in God's mathematics when one, plus one, plus one, equals three. Finally, there are times, times like today, when, one, plus one, plus one, equals one. Isn't God's math fun?

God takes one bride* and one groom* and adds them together. Then, out of pure love, God adds himself to them. One, plus one, plus one, and the total is one. One rope with three strands, all the strength needed for a lifetime together. In the "oneness" of our bride*, plus our groom*, plus God, there is strength without limit, love without limit, hope without limit, comfort without limit, forgiveness without limit, help without limit, and life without limit.

I am not sure God's way of doing math will work in our computers, but I am sure God's way of doing math works in our marriages. What God is adding together here today, one bride*, plus one groom*, plus God himself, let no one ever think of dividing apart.

Amen.

Joined Together
Matthew 19:3-6; 1 Corinthians 13

In speaking about marriage in the gospel of Matthew, Jesus said, "What God has joined together, let no one separate" (Matthew 19:6). Behind those words of our Lord there is much more than a rule for people to obey. Behind Jesus' words is a great truth for people to live by.

God joins people together. God joins people together with himself. God joins people together with each other. God joins people together with his promises. God joins people together with his creation.

We see that happening everywhere in the Bible. In the beginning we see God joining Adam to the very soil of his garden world. We see God joining flesh and bone together in the union of Adam and Eve. We see God joining himself with these newlyweds in the companionship that was life in Eden. Later in Genesis we see God joining Abraham together with three great promises upon which would be built the future of the whole human family. In Exodus we see God joining Moses together with the Hebrew people in one of history's great acts of deliverance.

In the gospels we see Jesus taking twelve men and joining them together into a community of faith, which has since opened and spread into the global Christian church. Also in the gospels, we see God's greatest act of joining people together. In Jesus God has joined himself forever to us. In Jesus God has joined himself to our sins, to our suffering, and to our death. In Jesus God has joined us to himself and to the love, forgiveness, goodness, life, and salvation that is in God, and that is God.

God joins people together. The adhesive God uses are all those things mentioned in the lessons read a few moments ago: love, kindness, forgiveness, humility, peace, servanthood, concern, gratitude, hope, faith, trust. Those are the things God uses when he joins us together with himself in Jesus. Those are the things God uses when he joins us together with one another, everywhere in life, and especially in marriage. Love, kindness, forgiveness, humility, peace, servanthood, concern, gratitude, hope, faith, and trust make up the God-created glue that joins couples together in marriage.

God joins people together. So important to God is that work of joining together that anything which breaks people apart must come from God's enemies. It was an enemy who broke Adam and Eve apart from God. It was an enemy who broke Adam and Eve apart from each other. It was an enemy who broke Adam and Eve apart from the goodness of the garden.

Breaking apart, wherever it occurs in the Bible, from the Garden of Eden to the crucifixion of Jesus, is the result of human partnership with the enemies of God. Breaking apart, wherever it occurs in life is a result of human partnership with the enemies of God and human refusal to give joining together God's priority.

John and Julie*, God wants you joined together. Give that same priority in your living that God gives. To keep your joining together strong, use the adhesive God supplies and that Jesus showed us so wonderfully how to use. Love each other. Be kind to each other. Forgive each other. Be humble servants to each other. Let peace, concern, gratitude, hope, faith, and trust exist everywhere in your life together.

Should anything ever happen to break you apart, remember that whatever it might be, it is the work of the enemies of God. Don't ever take their side. Take God's side in the joining of your lives together in marriage.

Amen.

Good Advice
Matthew 5:1-16

John and Julie*, since marriage is all about people living together here on God's good earth, I want to test your knowledge about other "earthly" things. What single crop is planted more and harvested in greater abundance than any other? What crop always has a market? What crop do some people give away for nothing, while others sell it for huge amounts of money?

The answer is advice. Everyone is in the advice-producing business, or so it seems, especially to people who are planning their wedding. The world produces advice in enormous quantities and on almost every subject. There is a constant demand for more. Advice books are far and away the best sellers of anything published. While old Ben down at the body shop gives away his homespun advice at absolutely no charge, his son, the psychologist, sells his advice for $200 an hour.

The human race is in the advice-producing business. Sometimes that is okay because we want and need advice. There are other times when what we want and what we need is not advice, but truth. No matter how people dress it up, advice is not the same as truth.

Today, at this wedding, we are gathered in the name of Jesus. The words of Jesus were read to us a few moments ago. Jesus is not an advice-dispenser. Jesus is a truth-giver. When any of us want truth instead of advice, there is no better person for us to listen to than Jesus.

John and Julie*, the scripture lesson from the fifth chapter of Matthew begins a section of the Bible called the Sermon on the Mount. Here Jesus is giving you the opportunity to build your life together not on the shifting sands of this world's advice, but on the solid rock of God's truth. Our prayers and our hopes are that you will succeed in doing that for yourselves, for each other, and for the good of all your brothers and sisters in the world. The human family doesn't need more people who live by following this world's advice. We are in desperate need of people whose lives are anchored in God's truth.

The world needs people who live by the truth Jesus provides in the scripture read today. The world needs people who admit their dependence upon God, who receive with joy those things they are given, and who in gratitude place their lives in the service of God's love. John and Julie*, in your life together in marriage be those kinds of people.

In a world hung up on the importance of having a good time, we need people who are willing to identify with the sorrow of their neighbors, people who are willing to listen to a problem, dry a tear, and help carry someone else's burden. In a world where aggressiveness is touted as the way to succeed, we need gentle people whose success is in their caring for humanity. In a world where money does too much of the talking, we need people to speak out on behalf of what is right, good, and just.

John and Julie*, in your life together, let your behavior be gentle and caring, and let your voices be strong in speaking out for justice.

When the advice of the world is to find out where others are vulnerable and attack them there, we need people who see where others are vulnerable and protect them there. When the advice of the world says we should use our freedom to make ourselves feel good, we need people who use their freedom not to feel good, but to do good. When the advice of the world is to defend yourself against all enemies, we need people who work for peace and for turning enemies into friends. In a world out of balance with bad advice, we need people bringing the strong weight of God's truth to set things right.

John and Julie*, in getting ready for your wedding I am sure you were given a lot of advice. Today Jesus has given you some good words of God's truth. The world is far from finished in giving you its advice. In your life together, you will need to stay close to God's truth. The world isn't helped much by married couples who spend their time listening to its advice. The help our world needs comes from married couples who spend their time living God's truth. John and Julie*, the world needs the two of you to live that kind of marriage.

Amen.

The Garden Is Gone
Mark 10:5-9

Marriage is for life. When God brought the man and the woman together in the garden, that was how marriage was meant to be. Marriage in the garden was to be a lifetime of companionship and mutual support. Marriage in the garden was to be a lifetime of two hearts beating in perfect harmony with each other and all creation. Marriage in the garden was to be a lifetime of two souls having perfect sensitivity to each other's needs, perfect joy in giving, and perfect delight in receiving. Marriage in the garden was to be a lifetime of two people never causing tears. Marriage in the garden was to be a lifetime when everything within each person, and everything within all of life around them, brought them closer together.

Everything about marriage in the garden was wonderful. How sad it is that the garden is gone. Marriage is so much more difficult for couples today because the garden is gone. John and Julie*, marriage will be more difficult for the two of you, because the garden is gone. For as long as people have been like us, for all of human memory, the garden has been gone. What is left, as far as marriage is concerned, is the reminder from our Lord that marriage is for life.

Marriage is for life. Yet so many of the elements that made lifetime marriage so easy and so perfect are no longer here. Humankind has squandered what our Creator had built into us. The loss is because of sin. What sin does in marriage is twist the life inside us and the life around us into shapes that drive husbands and wives apart. Sin replaces companionship with loneliness. Sin turns harmony into discord. Sin makes couples insensitive, eager to take, but reluctant to give. Sin leaves less of life to share and makes what is shared sometimes less than good. Sin at work in humankind has chopped away at the roots of lifetime marriage until the tree seems ready to topple.

It is all well and good to agree with Jesus and say that marriage is for life, but there remains a question for every married couple to answer. How can a garden marriage survive in a world where marriage has been so damaged by sin? John and Julie*, that is a question you must be able to answer. How can your garden marriage survive in the world you live in, a world where marriage is so damaged by sin?

The answer is that the two of you must work to make it survive. You must work against sin, wherever its effects show up, in your own lives and in the life of the world around you. The two of you must work to bring into your marriage all the goodness God intended for marriage when he established marriage in the garden.

The two of you must work to be true and good companions, always pushing life's not-good loneliness away from each other. The two of you must work in the fine tuning of your relationship to maintain and strengthen the precious harmony between you. The two of you must work to keep alive your sensitivity to each other's needs, so that you can give when your partner needs to receive, and receive when your partner needs to give. The two of you must work to ensure that what you do brings comfort, not pain. The two of you must work to keep the sharing going on in your individual experiences so that you go through life together, not allowing the pressures of life to drive you apart.

John and Julie*, when you pay careful attention to doing the work the goodness of your marriage requires, a garden marriage is possible for you, even in a world where the garden is gone. With the love and support you have from God, and with the love and support you can give to each other, you will have a marriage full of garden goodness. It will be the lifetime marriage Jesus wants you to have. All of us here today join our Lord in wanting the two of you to have a lifetime marriage, filled for a lifetime with God's garden goodness.

Amen.

Something New or Something Old
(Christmas Wedding)
Luke 2:1-20

John and Julie*, are you absolutely sure you want to go through with this marriage? You still have about six minutes to change your minds. After all, what are we talking about here? It is stuff like John being a husband, Julie being a wife. It's stuff like making a home, raising children, and becoming a family. It is stuff like loving, caring, helping, listening, and working together. All that sounds pretty old-fashioned to me, but I wonder, are you sure all of it isn't "out-of-date" in today's sophisticated world?

Out in the world people are talking about stuff like making big bucks, being good to yourself, state-of-the-art technology, owning the fanciest home and driving the coolest vehicle, vacationing in Italy and cruising in the Caribbean. That is "with it" stuff. That's the best the world has to offer. The two of you are capable, intelligent, good-looking people. You still have a chance to get in on that. You still have a chance to rise on that tide, go with that flow, and hit the jet-set jackpot.

Instead, here you are, planning to take up a lifestyle that was old-fashioned 2,000 years ago. Are you both sure that you are willing to settle for that? You are? Good! That puts you in awfully good company. That is also what God the Father was willing to settle for when he gave the world his Son.

God the Father certainly had a choice about where and when his Son was to be born. He could have chosen the Mayo Clinic instead of a Bethlehem stable. For his Son's father he could have chosen a Microsoft executive, instead of a self-employed carpenter. He could have chosen a woman from among the rich and famous to be the mother of the baby Jesus. Instead he chose from among the girls living in the small town of Nazareth. It was there he found a teenager with a faith and life that pleased him.

Instead of settling for a couple of scruffy shepherds as guests for the birth of the King of kings, God the Father could have flown in folks from Aspen and Palm Springs to get some media attention for the great event. The three kings gave the occasion some class, but why have them arrive by camel when they could have gotten to Bethlehem in Cadillacs? With a few careful choices, God the Father could have given Christmas night a lot more glamour than it had.

We can say the same thing about the choices God made for the raising of his Son. God could have arranged for private schools, a villa in Switzerland, and a crew of Rhodes scholars as tutors to train the boy. God had to know that it would be hard for Jesus to get into the best colleges when his school was a limestone-walled, dirt-floor workshop in nowhere Nazareth.

God the Father could have given his Son real celebrity status and everything that goes with it. Instead, he chose what was important to him; an ordinary, hardworking couple, husband and wife, for his Son's parents, a simple home in Nazareth, an ordinary family who did ordinary things, like loving each other, caring for each other, and helping each other. That was the kind of life God chose for his Son. That is the kind of life the two of you have chosen for yourselves.

Being a couple, loving each other, caring for each other, and helping each other might be old-fashioned, but it is still life at its best. I hope neither of you will ever think lightly of it. I hope the two of you will give to your marriage, to your home, to your family, to your love, and to your caring the same honor that God gave in the family of his Son.

Julie*, if you followed wedding tradition you have with you something old and something new. Your marriage today is both something new and something old. You are newlyweds entering a relationship that is as old as Adam and Eve, as Mary and Joseph. There is for you a lifetime of goodness when you take into your new life together the best of what is old: home and family, loving each other, helping each other, being good to each other.

Amen.

Home for Christmas
(Holiday Wedding)
Luke 15:11-24

During the holidays there is a lot of talk about home, "I'll be home for Christmas." "There is no place like home for the holidays." From Thanksgiving through Christmas, the pull of the holiday season draws people toward home.

But what is home? Is home to us the house in which we grew up? Maybe. Is it family? Is home to us the place where mom and dad are? Maybe. Or is home to us the place we go after work or after some activity? We look at our watches and say, "It's time to go home." Wherever we go after saying that, that place is home.

In Jesus' parable of the prodigal son, home was where dad was. Home was where dad was waiting, his arms open wide in welcome. Perhaps that is the real definition of home. Home is that place where someone waits for us with arms wide open in welcome.

For you and me, for a world of people who put their faith in Jesus as their Savior, home is heaven. Heaven is home for us because that is where God our Father waits for us, as with open arms he once waited for Jesus, his crucified and risen Son.

Home is where someone waits for us, their arms open wide in welcome. What a gift it is when the person with their arms open wide in welcome is our partner in marriage.

It has been a hard day. Things haven't gone well. You haven't handled yourself well. You're down on other people for the way they have acted. You're down on yourself for the way you have acted. You look at your watch. It's time to go home. When you get there your partner, your spouse, the person you married, is waiting for you, arms open wide in welcome. That's home!

Maybe you were not the nicest person to have been around in the morning before you left. On the way home you say to yourself, "I wonder if they are even going to want to talk to me, the way I acted." When you get home, you discover that it doesn't matter how you acted. On the other side of that door love is waiting for you. Love and welcome. That's home!

The gospel, the good news of what Jesus has accomplished for our salvation, tells us that it is going to be that way for us in heaven. For all our misbehavior, for all the times we have let God down, our heavenly Father is waiting for us in loving welcome.

In telling the parable of the prodigal son, Jesus is saying, "You can be like the father in the story." The two of you* can be like that for each other. Each of you can always know that when you get home you will be welcomed with open arms. Let that be the home each of you will be going to for the holidays and every day.

Amen.

Counting Costs
Luke 10:30-35

Love that does not count the cost. God's word tells us that this is the kind of love we ought to have for each other. Such love should be at its most generous, most self-forgetting, and most attuned to the well being of another in the marriage relationship.

That's the kind of love God is telling us to have in our marriages. The world around us doesn't seem to agree with God. The world around us thinks that counting the cost is a good thing. That is true if you are running a business. That is also true if you are operating a household. I suspect our couple* would agree that counting the cost has been an important part of planning their wedding. What is necessary in some parts of our living is not necessary and does not even belong, in others areas, especially in marriage.

Counting the cost is something the world wants husbands and wives to do. The world wants husbands and wives to make sure they are getting as much out of their marriage as they are putting into it. "Count the cost." That's what I hear the world saying. "Make sure you are getting at least your share." "Don't stay in a marriage unless you know you are getting everything you deserve out of that marriage." So many people not staying in their marriages is sad evidence that people are listening to what the world is telling them.

God is telling us, telling the two of you, something different. God is telling each of you, every husband and wife here today, not to count the cost as you live your marriage. Don't be concerned about getting what you think you deserve from your partner. Instead, be eager to give everything you have to your partner.

In the gospel lesson you included in your wedding and the parable of the good Samaritan, Jesus tells us what it means to be a neighbor. Being a neighbor means that you don't count the cost when it comes to giving another person the help they need. Although Jesus doesn't say it, being a husband or a wife means the same. Being a husband or a wife means you don't count the cost in giving your partner the help, love, support, encouragement, forgiveness, happiness, companionship, and goodness of life they need. Those are things you just do, because giving those things without counting the cost is what marriage is all about.

There are places in the Bible in which God describes his relationship to us as a relationship of husband and wife. God knows what we need: his love, forgiveness, salvation. In giving us Jesus, he gives us those things without counting the cost. He does it because our relationship means that much to him.

God grant that your relationship means that much to each of you. In giving us Jesus, God gave his best to us. So give your best to each other. If you are going to count the cost, let it be in things like paying the bills from your wedding and not in living the lifetime of love in your marriage.

Amen.

Don't Worry
Luke 12:22-31

Wedding days are great occasions, full of happiness, hope, family, and friends taking time to share together in prayer, praise, food, fun, and conversation. A wedding day is one of life's good days. But, there is, on the far edges of our feelings, a little worry. Marriages are going through tough times in today's world. Every one of us has seen many that haven't survived. We worry. We all worry. Will this marriage work? We think it will. We pray that it will. We want it to work. We are going to do everything we can to make it work, but will it? Will our bride and groom* really be happy? Will the two of them grow closer together in the years to come? They are so young. What do they really know about life? What do they really know about each other? What about money? What about the host of problems that are certain to arise? Will they be able to handle those problems and stay together?

I don't know about the rest of you, but the more I think about it, the more worried I become. John and Julie* are you sure you want to go through with this?

"Don't worry." That is what Jesus is saying in the scripture lesson that was read a few moments ago. "Do not worry about your life," Jesus says (Luke 12:22 NRSV). Then he tells us that our concern is to be for the kingdom of God and doing what God requires of us. God will look after the rest of our lives.

What would be wrong with taking Jesus at his word? Jesus is right, of course. Worry doesn't add a thing to the goodness of life. Planning does. Caring does. Loving does. Working does. Laughing does. Maybe even crying does. Goodness happens when we share one another's tears. There are many things we can do to add to the goodness of our lives. Worrying is not one of them.

Jesus does not promise that if we focus our attention on the kingdom of God and quit worrying about stuff, all our troubles will disappear. I wish I could say that to our couple*. I suspect that is something our couple* would like to hear, that they have Jesus' guarantee of a lifetime together without any problems or trouble. I can't say that. Jesus doesn't say that.

What Jesus does say is that God cares very deeply about our bride and groom*. God cares very deeply about every person here. Every person in the world, including our bride and groom*, and you and I, is precious to God. God cares about us. Jesus wants us to know that every day of our lives God is with us with all his love and with all his care.

Because Jesus shared our lives with us, Jesus knows from experience that trouble happens. It is part of being human. Through Jesus, the time will come when God will lift the whole human family out of all its troubles. That time is not yet. Trouble happens. It happened to Jesus. It happens to us.

God grant that our couple* will be spared the worst kinds of trouble in their life together. That is our hope and our prayer. We know they will have some trouble. We know, and we want them to know, that the God who gives his blessing to their marriage will be there with them and for them every day of their married life. God will be there on those days when trouble happens. God will be there to listen. God will be there to comfort. God will be there to support. God will be there to encourage. God will be there to get them through.

When Mary Magdalene came to Jesus with tears in her eyes, Jesus dried those tears and brought a smile to Mary's face. John and Julie*, on those days when you come to Jesus with tears in your eyes he will do the same for you. Jesus wants you both to know that. All the people here celebrating this good day with you want you both to know that.

Let us all join our couple* in taking Jesus at his word. As they are putting their marriage in God's hands and trusting in his care, let us all do the same with our lives. Let us give the best of our attention to living faithfully to God and faithfully to each other. As John and Julie* begin each day of their marriage knowing God will be there in that day, with them and for them, let us all begin our days with that same confidence.

"Don't worry," Jesus says. Knowing that John and Julie's* marriage, and your life and mine, are safe and secure in the hands of God makes this good day even better.

Amen.

New Beginnings
Luke 7:11-17

In the scripture lesson just read, we are told how Jesus brought life back to a young man who had died. New life for the young man, and new life, lively and joyful, to the dead ashes of a mother's heart. New life, warm and loving, to a relationship fatally fractured by the power of death.

Those who had witnessed Jesus' miracle call out in response, "God has shown his care for his people" (Luke 7:16 Revised English Bible). God has shown his care by taking that which was dead, lost, gone, destroyed, and bringing it back to life with a whole new future of opportunities and possibilities spreading out before it.

God cares. God cares about people. God cares about you and me. God cares about us on days like today, when our lives are filled with happiness. God cares about us on those other days, when our lives are filled with sorrow. God cares about the well-being of our bodies. God cares about the well-being of our hearts, minds, and souls. God cares about the well-being of our relationships. God shows his care by taking that which is dead and bringing it back to life.

Without God's care, life would not have any chance at all in our world. Without God's care, our relationships with each other would not survive. Without God's care, our marriages would not survive. We human beings have a well-developed ability to make things dead. The ruins of destroyed relationships are all around us. We know how to make things dead. Only God knows how to take that which is dead and bring it back to life.

Our God is a God who exalts in giving life. Our God is a God who exalts in building relationships. God knows far better than you and I how important relationships are to us. While we can taunt the monster of loneliness and despair with our cavalier treatment of one another, play those marital games of seeing how far we can bend the relationship without breaking it, God is working to undo the damage we have caused. God heals and restores the relationships on which the happiness of our lives, and the well-being of our world, depend. Where there should be death, God opens life. God doesn't ask us if we want it. God does it because he knows we need it.

John and Julie*, today, your wedding day, you both know how important God's care is for you and for this new relationship of yours in marriage. God's care is going to be even more important in the days, weeks, months, and years to come. God is the one who will keep your relationship alive. God is the one who will take what might seem to be ending and create for it a whole new beginning. When all you can see before you are closed doors in your life together, God is the one who will open those doors providing new opportunities for you to explore what it means to love, care for, and sacrifice for one another.

God shows his care by bringing new life to that which is dead. At those times when God does that for you in your marriage, embrace that new life. Let go of what has ended. Take hold of God's new beginnings. Explore every opportunity God's care will open for you to find new goodness in your marriage. God is here today as your marriage is coming to life. Because God knows how much you need each other, God will always be there in your marriage, creating those new beginnings that keep your relationship fresh and alive.

Amen.

Ordinary Things
(Christmas Wedding)
Luke 2:8-12

Jesus' birth is the greatest event in the history of the world. The Creator of the universe enters his creation. God becomes one with us to save us from ourselves. In Jesus' birth, God is laying aside his eternal life to be with us in our mortal death, bringing humankind out of death to life, his life, God's eternal life. Jesus' birth is so overwhelming that all the great events of human history pale in significance beside it. The best of human accomplishments are nothing compared to what God accomplished in the birth of his Son.

One of the things that is so marvelous about the Christmas story is that it didn't take place among the rich and famous. There are no chauffeured limousines in the Christmas story, no superstars invited, no doctors flown in from Switzerland to attend the birth, no red carpets, and no crowd of television trucks aiming dishes into the sky beaming broadcasts to satellites in outer space.

The most extraordinary event in all of history comes to us clothed in the most ordinary of things: shepherds, straw, a stable, a manger, a towel or two. On a dark night in a small town, in a scene little different from uncountable others on the planet earth, a mother is cradling her newborn baby. Standing beside them a man looks on with love, hoping he can give the two of them the care they need in a world that can be very cold and cruel.

Like the water of our baptism, like the bread and wine of the sacramental meal, Christmas helps us understand that God is there even in the most common and ordinary things. Nothing in all creation is too small or ordinary to carry God's blessing. All things, even the most common, participate in God's miracle of life.

Although wedding days are often filled with much that is uncommon and extraordinary, marriage itself is made up of ordinary things.

That is not its weakness. That is its strength. The ordinary things of marriage carry God's blessings for you, and God's blessings from you. A simple smile, a positive word of encouragement, a quiet moment to listen and talk, to make plans for a weekend, share a dinner with family and friends, sing together at worship, pray together at home, and do what good neighbors do for those who need your help, all these are the ordinary things, the common things of life together in marriage. That is where the love of God, and the miracle of Christ, take place in you, between you, and through you.

John and Julie*, don't give your hearts to what you could make extraordinary in your marriage: big money, big homes, big cars, important friends, fabulous vacations, successful careers. Those can be empty things, like the king's palace on the night Jesus was born. Treasure the ordinary things in your married life like the moments you share, the words you share, the things you discover about each other, the work you do to keep your marriage good, the work you do to raise a family where goodness is shared as daily bread.

That is all stable-and-straw kind of stuff but that's where God's blessing is. When you give your best to the common and ordinary things in your life together, you will have a marriage envied by angels and kings.

Amen.

I Have Called You Friends
John 15:15

"I have called you friends." That is what our Lord Jesus said to his disciples in John 15:15 (NRSV). How good it is to have a friend! That's what today and tomorrow are about, the goodness that is ours because of the friends we have. Tomorrow morning a group of people will gather here in this place to celebrate the very special friend the world has, and the very special friend they have, in Jesus.

"What a friend we have in Jesus." We have a friend who loves us. Jesus loves us with a wonderful love that does not take away our freedom or smother our identity. Jesus' love liberates us. We are never more free than when we are loved by Jesus!

"What a friend we have in Jesus." We have a friend who prays for us. Think of it. Wherever we go, whatever we do, we always know that someone is speaking to God the Father on our behalf. That someone is Jesus!

"What a friend we have in Jesus." He gives himself to us in that miraculous way in which he becomes one with us, and we become one with him. Through our union with Jesus, we are joined forever to God, and God is joined forever to us.

"What a friend we have in Jesus. All our sins and grief to bear." There is nothing we cannot talk about when we talk to him. Jesus always understands us. Jesus always accepts us as we are. When we ask for his forgiveness, we know our Lord Jesus will give it to us. When we talk to him about our disappointments, about how down we are feeling, Jesus always lifts us up.

"What a friend we have in Jesus." He never competes with us. Instead, Jesus cheers us on, encouraging us, bringing out the very best in us as children of God. "What a friend we have in Jesus." He gave his own life and died on the cross for us, so that you and I, his friends, will live forever! Jesus is the kind of friend who never forgets us and never leaves us behind. When Jesus does go on ahead, he does so "to get things ready" for us. Whenever we wonder about our future, we know one thing for sure, wherever we go, whatever happens, Jesus will be there as our friend!

How good it is to have a friend, a special friend. Tomorrow, here in this place, we will be celebrating the special friendship we have with Jesus. Today, in this place, we are celebrating the special friendship these two people* have in each other.

In a moment they* will be exchanging vows. When you listen carefully to what they are saying, you will hear in their words, the words the disciples heard from Jesus, "I call you friend"; wife — yes, husband — yes, but also, friend.

How good it is to have a friend. How good it is to have a special friend. How good it is that these two people* have each other as the best of friends.

How good it is that each of them has a friend who loves them with a love that does not want to control or smother them but sets them free to celebrate who they are, and what they have in their life together.

How good it is that each of them has a friend who prays for them, including their hopes and dreams, their joys and sorrows, in each day's quiet conversations with a God who listens and who cares.

How good it is that in each other they are experiencing the miracle of "oneness." Two friends seeing life through a single pair of eyes. Two friends feeling life through a single heart.

How good it is that in each other they have a friend who listens. A friend who can hear more than just words being spoken. A friend who can see the soul being shared.

How good it is that in each other they have found a companion, not a competitor; a friend who cheers them on, encouraging them to be the very best that they can be in everything they do.

How good it is that in each other they have found a friend who has for them what Jesus calls the greatest love of all. A friend who will not only live with them, but who will, if need be, die for them.

How good it is that in each other they have found a friend who will never leave them behind. A friend who will always be there with them and for them no matter what.

How good, how wonderful, it is to have a friend. How good, how wonderful, it is to have a special friend. What a joy it is that the world has that kind of friend in Jesus! What a joy it is these two people* have that kind of friend in each other!

Amen.

Love
John 3:16, 13:34, 13:35, 15:13, 21:17;
1 Corinthians 13:13; 1 John 4:19;
Ephesians 5:25; Song of Solomon 4:10

One word sums up the scripture lessons being read today. That word is "love"! The Bible is full of the word "love." In one biblical book after another, on one page in the Bible after another, love is written about and celebrated.

Sometimes the Bible rejoices over the wonderful truth of God's love for us. "For God so loved the world that he gave his only Son, so that everyone who believes in [Jesus] may not perish but may have eternal life" (John 3:16).

Sometimes the Bible talks about our love for Jesus. "Do you love me?" Jesus asks his disciple Peter. Peter answers, not only for himself, but also for you and me. "Lord," he says, "you know everything; you know that I love you" (John 21:17).

Sometimes the Bible talks about love in the church. "By this," says our Lord, "everyone will know that you are my disciples, if you have love for one another" (John 13:35).

Sometimes the Bible presents love at its deepest expression. Again it is Jesus who describes what that kind of love is like. "No one has greater love than this," he tells and shows us, "to lay down one's life for one's friends" (John 15:13).

Sometimes the Bible teaches about love and about where love has its beginning, as a gift from God, "Faith, hope and love, these three [gifts of God's Holy Spirit] abide. The greatest [of God's gifts] is love" (1 Corinthians 13:13).

Sometimes the Bible allows us to see our own love as the mirror image of the love of God. "We love because [God] first loved us" (1 John 4:19).

Sometimes stressing how crucial love is in our often love-starved world, the Bible makes love a command. "Love one another!" (John 13:34).

There are also times the Bible places love where we see and celebrate it today, right in the center of married life, "Husbands, love your wives!" (Ephesians 5:25), and as the poet groom of the Song of Solomon writes, "Your love delights me, my sweetheart and my bride" (Song of Solomon 4:10 GNB).

Love is everywhere in the Bible. Our Bibles are crowded with love. What these two people* need to do and want to do is to get all the love that is everywhere in this book, everywhere in their marriage. What all of us here need to do and want to do is to get the love that is everywhere in our Bibles, everywhere in our own lives, and everywhere in our own marriages.

We can write down what the Bible says about love on plaques for our walls and magnets for our refrigerators. That's okay, but you might not always be standing in front of the refrigerator when your love is needed. The wall plaque might be in the wrong room.

The best way to get all the love in the Bible into our living, into our marriages, into our families, is to put our lives, marriages, and families into the Bible. We do that by taking up the Bible's story of love in the story of our own living. We do what the Bible does; live our lives accepting God's gift of love, celebrating God's gift of love, loving God, loving Jesus, loving others, loving our partners in marriage and family, loving when love comes easily, loving when love comes hard, loving when love gives you everything you want, loving when love costs you everything you have. That is the story of love as the Bible tells it.

The two of you*, take up the Bible's story of love in your life together. As love is everywhere in the Bible, let love be everywhere in your marriage. From today's first chapter to the last word on the last page of the story of the two of you*, let love be everywhere!

Amen!

To Heal as Jesus Did
(Two Physical Therapists' Wedding)
John 5:1-9; Psalm 100; Colossians 3:12-17; John 15:9-17

Every wedding is unique, but this wedding is even more so. What makes it unique is that we have not just one physical therapist getting married. We have two physical therapists getting married to each other. That being the case, it seems appropriate that one of the scripture lessons being read today should be about physical therapy. Since you didn't include one, I did from the gospel of John 5:1-9.

The setting for Jesus' miracle of healing, the pool at Bethzatha, bears a powerful resemblance to the physical therapy unit in a hospital. There are physically impaired people waiting for treatment. There is a therapy pool, which seems to have had a kind of angelic jacuzzi function to it. There is the crippled man with his mat, and there is the therapist. In this case, the therapist is Jesus.

In our gospel text, Jesus diagnoses the cause of the disability and successfully treats it. The crippled man's mobility is restored. He leaves the unit not only walking but carrying his mat with him. Like everything else he does, when Jesus heals he does it well. That is a model for John and Julie* in their careers. That is also a model for John and Julie* in their marriage, to not only do those things, but to do them well.

We can assume that it was in medical school that John and Julie* learned to do that in their careers. They learned how to do the work of physical therapy, and they learned how to do it well. Life has taught John and Julie* about doing the work of marriage. The scripture lesson they included in their wedding teaches them, and us, how to do that work of marriage, and how to do it well.

It begins with living by the virtues Paul describes to the Colossians: gentleness, kindness, humility, meekness, patience, willingness to forgive, concern for establishing peace in the marriage relationship, and a commitment to love each other. Couples who do those things in their lives together as husbands and wives not only do the work of building their marriages, but do it well.

The scripture lessons go on. Psalm 100 celebrates the praise to God that is so much a part of our living as God's people. "Make a joyful noise to the Lord, all the earth. Worship the Lord with gladness; come into his presence with singing" (Psalm 100:1-2). The Apostle Paul echoes the Psalmist, "With gratitude in your hearts sing psalms, hymns, and spiritual songs to God" (Colossians 3:16). Husbands and wives who bring that praise-based spirit of faith and worship to their life not only do the work of building their marriages, but they do it well.

The gospel lesson our couple has included in their wedding goes on to an even higher level. The best, the greatest, way to do the work of building a marriage, and to do it well, is to love not only as people do, but to love as Jesus loves. That is to love with a love that never asks for itself, but gives all for the other. Couples who bring that Christ-like love to their life together not only do the work of building their marriages, but they do it well.

John and Julie,* in your careers Jesus has invited you to join him in his ministry of healing, to heal as he does and to do it well. Today, as you begin your married life, Jesus invites himself, through the Holy Spirit, into your relationship as husband and wife. Jesus is with you as you do the work of building your marriage. With his excellent gifts and his strong support, you will certainly be able to do all the work your marriage is ever going to need, and do it well.

Amen.

Love:
Commanded and Encouraged
John 15:12

Our society celebrates love as a spontaneous emotion. A man and a woman, our bride and groom* for example, glance toward each other across a crowded room. Their eyes meet. Suddenly bells are chiming, birds are singing, silly, and sappy expressions cover their faces. They are in love!

Following that heart-melting moment they each shop for the best deodorant, stock up on mouthwash, pay extra attention to the kind of shampoo they use, and do all they can to make themselves as irresistible to each other as humanly possible. This leads them to engagement and marriage.

Being married, our couple rents an apartment, applies for a Visa card, makes the choice about which to have first — a dog or a baby, and lives happily ever after. Our couple lives happily ever after, that is, until one of them falls out of love. What began with their eyes meeting across that crowded room ends with them signing legal papers across a lawyer's desk.

That is love as our society defines it. The Bible sees love differently. There is, in the Bible, the joy and spontaneity of falling in love. The chiming bells, singing birds, and sappy expressions are celebrated in the Song of Solomon as one of the wonders of human living, a special gift of the God who, as the Apostle Paul writes, "richly provides us with everything for our enjoyment" (1 Timothy 6:17).

Two people falling in love is as treasured in the Bible as it is in the movies. God delights in people falling in love, but God wants even more for people to act in love and to make love the determining factor in how they treat one another in marriage and in life.

In our gospel text, Jesus does not say, "fall in love with each other." What Jesus does say is, "love one another" (John 15:12). He doesn't just say it as the kind of advice a couple might receive from a wedding guest in the receiving line. Jesus orders us to do it. "This is my commandment," he says, "that you love one another" (John 15:12). Jesus goes on to make it clear what our love is to be like. "Love one another as I have loved you" (John 15:12).

God may delight in people falling in love, but God is not pleased with people falling out of love in marriage or in life. To love each other, day in and day out, week after week, year after year, is something God commands us to do. Everywhere in God's word we are provided with the encouragement we need to keep Jesus' command to love in the center of our lives. "Beloved, let us love one another" (1 John 4:7), John writes to the church, to our couple*, and to each one of us. Our couple* and you and I are to love one another as Jesus loves us.

For our couple*, the love that began with chiming bells, singing birds, and sappy expressions, leads into love that is all about caring, helping, listening, encouraging, supporting, forgiving, and being for each other the lifelong companion God created them each to be. God commands and encourages them to have that kind of love for each other. God commands and encourages every husband and wife to have that kind of love for each other. God commands and encourages every person here to have that kind of love for all our neighbors everywhere in his world.

John and Julie*, all of us are so happy that the two of you fell in love. God is happy about that too. We join God in our strong hope that what happens so often in the movies never happens in your marriage and that neither one of you ever falls out of love. Our prayer is that you will always love each other the way your Lord and Savior has always loved you. Never stop loving each other. Your family and friends, gathered here today, promise to never stop loving you.

Amen.

Marriage Advice
John 15:9-16

John and Julie*, this very special day belongs to the two of you. For years to come, whenever anyone here thinks about this date, they will say to themselves, "That was the day John and Julie* were married." The two of you have suddenly become VIPs. There are guests who have traveled long distances to see you, honor you, and pay their respects to you. Most of those people have even brought you gifts. Why is it, then, when the two of you are the most important people here today, everyone who has anything to say feels quite free to tell you what to do?

Does the photographer stand where you tell him to stand? Oh, no. You are at the mercy of his orders. You can't even tip your heads the way you want. He will tell you how to stand, smile, tip your heads, and what to look at. After the photographer come the personal attendants, bridesmaids, groomsmen, your parents, your relatives, and your friends. Have you noticed? They aren't listening to what you tell them. They are way too busy with what they have to tell you. As you already know, I am right there with them.

One piece of wedding advice no one needs to tell you today is that you must love each other. That is something you already know how to do. The fact that you love each other has brought you here today. The songs that are sung today are songs you chose to tell your guests about your love for each other. The vows you speak to each other today are your public witness to the commitment born in your private love for each other. The candle you light today symbolizes a oneness in your relationship that is rooted in the love each of you has grown to have for the other.

One thing no one tells you, or dares to tell you, is that you must love each other. Your love for each other is written all over this whole day. We are here to celebrate with you the marvelous and joyful reality that you have made us so aware of: The two of you really do love each other.

Our Lord is here with you today. Jesus is here to celebrate with you the goodness of today. Jesus is here to bless you on this good day and to bring God's blessing to all the days, weeks, months, and years of your life together. Jesus is also here to tell you to love each other. The words from the gospel of John, which you have chosen to be included in your wedding, are Jesus' words. They are his words of command. Jesus tells you to "love one another" (John 15:12 NRSV). Jesus says, "John and Julie*, I am telling to love each other."

Maybe you don't need Jesus to tell you that today, but you will in the days to come. There are going to be days when both of you are tired from some project you are doing at home. You are hot and sweaty and not just a little cranky. On days like that Jesus will be there telling you, "John and Julie*, I want you to love each other." Not only will Jesus be telling you that but he will also expect you to listen to him and do what he says.

When things go wrong between the two of you and all sorts of cracks are opening up in your relationship, you'll wonder if getting married was such a good idea. Jesus will be there in those times, giving you the only marriage advice you really need to hear, "John and Julie*," Jesus will say, "I want you to love each other." Jesus will expect both of you to pay attention to that advice and to do what he says.

In a few hours this day will be over. All those people who have been telling you what to do are going to back off and be quiet. They know that they no longer have any business giving you advice. You are going to be glad they do that. Be glad Jesus doesn't.

Every day of your marriage Jesus is going to be there giving you his advice and his orders. On every good day and every bad day, Jesus is going to be there saying, "John and Julie*, love each other. This is my commandment, that you love one another as I have loved you" (John 15:12).

Every night, when you have listened to Jesus and obeyed his command, putting your love to work to maintain the goodness of your life together, you will go to sleep with a prayer of thanks on your lips. "Thank you, Lord Jesus. Thank you for being here today with your marriage advice, telling us what you knew we needed to be told. You want us to love each other. We listened. We have. We do. Amen."

Be glad you no longer will have people telling you what to do for your wedding. Be gladder still that you will always have Jesus telling you what to do for your marriage. "John and Julie*, love each other."

Amen.

Jesus Is With You
John 6:1-14

John and Julie*, I am not going to give you a lecture on what married life should be like. Another thing I am not going to do is preach a sermon on the doctrines of the church regarding marriage. What I am going to do is show you a person, the person who was there with all those hungry people in Galilee, the person who gave that crowd of 5,000 families the food they needed. The person I want you to see is Jesus. As Jesus was with those people when they needed him, so Jesus will be with you in your marriage when you need him.

"I am with you always" (Matthew 28:20), Jesus said to his disciples, to his church, and to us. Jesus is with you today. Jesus will be with you tomorrow. Jesus will be with you in all the days, weeks, months, and years of your life together in marriage. See him. Know him. Jesus has so much love for both of you. Every day you can relearn how to love each other from the love you experience from him.

Jesus wants the best for both of you in your marriage. As the hungry people in Galilee didn't have to convince Jesus to help them have a good meal, neither do you have to convince Jesus to help you have a good marriage. Jesus already wants to do that. Jesus already cares about your marriage. Jesus already wants your marriage to be the best he can help you make it be. Your marriage has no better friend than Jesus. With his support and encouragement, your marriage can survive life's hardest blows. You can face anything together, because you have Jesus with you and you have each other.

Jesus is with you today. Know Jesus' forgiveness for you. Know how much you each need that forgiveness and know how freely Jesus gives it. Be generous in sharing with each other the forgiveness you receive from him. Jesus will be there in your marriage and your family giving you all the forgiveness you will ever need.

John and Julie*, Jesus will be there with you in your marriage, just as Jesus is here with you at your wedding. Know him. Know his promises. Know the hope and the joy Jesus brings to your lives. Know his touch. Let his touch heal you, restore you, free you, and encourage you. Feel Jesus' hand always there on your joined hands. As Jesus' hand broke the bread and fed the multitude, so will his hand create miracles in your life together.

John and Julie*, see Jesus with you in your marriage. Know that he will always be there for you, providing what you need to have the marriage he knows you want.

Amen.

Miracles in Marriage
John 2:1-11

When we read the story of the wedding at Cana, our attention is first drawn to the miracle itself: changing water into wine, and then, perhaps, to the astonishing quantity of wine produced by it. That must have been some wedding reception! We could go on to speculate about the taste of the miracle wine. Was there an usual or unnatural taste or did it have the flavor of grapes and ground, of sunshine and rain, and the feet of the grape stompers? Another consideration in the story could be the relationship of Jesus to his mother. There is that sharp edge in Jesus' response to her which makes us wonder.

One part of the story we might miss but is of considerable importance to what is happening here today is that this miracle was the first miracle Jesus performed. The miracle was done at the ceremony beginning a marriage. I believe in these days there are few places where the miracles of God are needed more than in marriage and family.

So many things today seem set on destroying the marriage relationship. When marriages are in pain, families are in pain. Good, strong marriages and good, happy families depend upon two people loving each other, day after day, week after week, month after month, year after year, through all the circumstances of life. When that happens in today's world, it is no less a miracle of God than Jesus turning water into wine at that wedding in Cana.

If we want to see miracles in our world, we don't need to look for people throwing away their crutches or having their malignant tumors disappear. All we need to look for are people being kind to each other in the morning when they get up, in the evening when they go bed, and in their moments together in between. Kindness as a daily way of life in a marriage. That's a miracle!

If we want to see miracles in our world, we don't need to look for people surviving accidents without injury. All we need to look for are people forgetting about themselves and what they want and helping another person get what that person needs. Self-giving as a daily way of life in marriage. That's a miracle!

If we want to see miracles in our world, we don't need to look for people who are unable to pay their rent finding a winning lottery ticket. All we need to look for are people sharing with one another the daily bread of forgiveness. When, instead of letting the grudges and injuries of the past destroy the present, people in marriages and families continually offer each other new days for new beginnings. That's a miracle!

If we want to see miracles in our world, we don't need to look for people living to be 120 years old. All we need to look for are people who are more interested in the quality of their living together than in the quantity of what they are able to buy together. Marriages where bigger hearts are more important than bigger homes are a miracle!

Everywhere marriage and family life is being lived as God created it to be lived, delivering daily goodness to people's lives, there are miracles happening. When husbands and wives invite God to work in their life together, and when husbands and wives participate together with God in working for the goodness of their marriage, miracles are going to happen just as surely as the miracle happened at the wedding in Cana.

John and Julie*, our prayer today is that those miracles will be part of your married life. We hope and pray that you will seek those miracles from God, and that you will participate in them by your ongoing care for the goodness of your life together. May it be that when we look to see those miracles, which happen when God is at work in the world, we need look no further than your marriage.

Amen.

Connections
John 15:1-17

John and Julie*, to live well in this world you have to make the right connections. I mean that exactly the way it sounds. To live well in this world you have to get connected. You have to get your plumbing connected, your electricity, your telephone, and your sewer. I can promise that if those things are not connected, you are not going to live well.

You know that, of course. When you checked out the place in which you are living, you made sure all the connections were made. The lights go on when you flip the switch. The water that comes out of the cold water faucet isn't hot. When things disappear down the drain they don't show up again on the basement floor. No one needs to tell you that those connections are important.

Hopefully you know that in your life together in marriage your connection with Jesus is just as important. As much as living well requires those things that flow into your home through the connections that have been made with public utilities, living well as husband and wife requires those things that flow into your lives through the connections that have been made with Jesus.

Through those connections, Jesus' forgiveness flows into your life together. To live well in marriage you need that forgiveness to give to each other. It will be daily bread for your married life. Through your connections with Jesus, hope flows into your life together. To live well in marriage you need that hope to share with each other. It will give its brightness to a future that on some days might seem very dark. Through your connections with Jesus, healing power flows into your life together. To live well in marriage you need the touch of Jesus to continually renew and recreate the goodness of your married life. Through your connections with Jesus, faith, courage, and strength flow into you to use on behalf of your life together. To live well in marriage you will need faith in

God and in each other. To live well in marriage you need courage and strength to stand together against all those things that will try to tear you apart.

Best of all, flowing into your life together, is love. Love is God's best gift given to you by the Holy Spirit through your connections with Jesus. Love with its kindness, gentleness, humility, and patience — love as only God can give it — will make your marriage a place where both of you will spend a lifetime living well.

John and Julie*, all sorts of connections need to be made as you begin your life together. You know how important each of those connections is. In the scripture lesson for your wedding, Jesus is telling you how important your connections are with him. Live close to him, close to his word, close to Jesus' presence in his church, pour out your prayers to him, as he pours out himself to you. To live well in marriage, your connections with Jesus are the most important connections you will ever have.

Amen.

Abiding in Love
John 15:9-13; John 13:34

"If you keep my commandments, you will abide in my love" (John 15:10).

John and Julie*, how can the two of you keep your love for each other alive in this world? I doubt I am revealing any hidden secret when I say that the world seems to delight in providing us all sorts of reasons not to love each other. We are presented with endless opportunities to be angry with each other. We are given crystal clear vision of each other's flaws and faults. We are bumblingly incapable of hiding our own flaws and faults. Jealousy breaks down our trust. Pride breaks down our tenderness. Casualness breaks down our commitments. We misunderstand each other. We wrong each other. We disappoint each other.

Through all that, we are expected to keep our love for each other alive. That this is not so easy is evidenced by the growing list of marriages ending in divorce. How can people, John and Julie*, how can the two of you keep love for each other alive in this kind of world?

Jesus provides a way to help the two of you keep your love. "If you keep my commandments," Jesus says, "you will abide in my love" (John 15:10). John and Julie*, if you obey Jesus' commandments, you will have Jesus' love to live in and to share.

When you give priority in your life together to Jesus' commandments, you will forget about yourself and the way you want things to be. What will be important is how Jesus wants things to be. When you give priority in your life together to Jesus' commandments, you will forget about the world and the way the world tells you things should be. What will be important is the way Jesus says things should be.

"I give you a new commandment, that you love one another. Just as I have loved you, you also should love one another" (John

13:34). That is Jesus' commandment that you love one another with the same love Jesus has for you. When you make a mistake, Jesus still loves you. Jesus sees all your faults and flaws, and he still loves you. When you disappoint Jesus, Jesus still loves you. When you fail to pay attention to Jesus, fail to honor him and respect him as you should, Jesus still loves you. When you fail to keep a promise to Jesus, Jesus still keeps his promise and loves you. When you want more from Jesus than you are willing to give to Jesus, Jesus still loves you.

That is the kind of love Jesus has always had and will always have for you. When you make it the priority in your life together to have that same kind of love for each other, his love, which is alive and well within you, will be alive and well in your marriage. The world, and all the reasons it will give you for not loving each other, won't matter. What will matter are all the reasons Jesus gives you to abide in his love and let his love abide in your marriage.

Amen.

Love in the Afternoon
John 15:12-16

"Love one another" (John 15:12). That is what our Lord Jesus tells us to do. That is what Jesus says, and that is what this afternoon is about. It is about love. The two of you, John and Julie*, are living within the warm, creative, saving embrace of God's love for you. Your family and your friends, all those here with you today, are living in the same embrace of that love of God.

Living in God's love gives us a sense of joy, peace, and hope, which adds a richness and a wonder to all of life's events. It is God's love that provides the background against which this wedding is taking place. Without that love, everything about this afternoon would be so much less.

Love is what this afternoon is all about. We are living in the marvelous good-news reality of God's love for people. We are living as the people God loves by loving one another. John and Julie*, what has gathered these people together is not the persuasiveness of your invitation or the compelling aroma of the reception meal. What has brought these people here to share this afternoon with you is the magnetic effect of your love for each other. They are here to witness that love and to share it with you.

Love is what this afternoon is about. This afternoon is about our living in God's love. This afternoon is about celebrating your love. This afternoon is about all of us being open to God's guidance in our being better lovers of each other and better lovers of all our brothers and sisters in the world.

This afternoon is about our listening to Jesus as he tells us to "love one another." This afternoon is about love that does not ebb and flow according to our emotions. It is about love that remains strong and constant, day after day, week after week, month after month, anniversary after anniversary, and crisis after crisis. It is about love that is not anchored in our flimsy spirits, but in Jesus' powerful command. We are better lovers when our emotions are undergirded and stabilized by the words of our Lord. Every married couple at this wedding knows that love is too important to be left only to the feelings of the moment. The moments of our lives belong to Jesus. Every moment is under his command to us to "love one another."

Love is what this afternoon is all about, living in God's love, celebrating your love, and being open to God's guidance so that we can be better lovers. We could talk about love as sacrifice. "Love one another as I have loved you" (John 15:12), says Jesus. The love of Jesus is love not as receiving but love as giving. It is love that finds its joy not in how good things are for us, but in how good we can make things for another. Better lovers are those who give more than they receive.

We can talk about love as partnership in God's creation. Love as being God's people together and doing God's work together. God's work, the task he placed us in the world to do, is the tending and nurturing work of bringing the goodness of creation to blossom so that all can enjoy it. Better lovers are those who do love's work together as companions.

Love is what this afternoon is all about. John and Julie*, may love be what the years of your marriage are all about. Live in God's love, always. Celebrate your love, always. Always be open to God's guidance for your being better lovers toward each other and toward God's world.

Amen.

A Successful Marriage
Romans 12:1-21

What does it take for a person to live a successful life? Is it possible for two people, each striving to be a success in life, to have a successful marriage? It depends. It depends on who those two people are listening to, the wisdom of the world or the word of God. Julie and John*, the scripture lesson you have chosen to be read at your wedding, Romans 12, describes the secret of living a successful life very differently than the wisdom of the world. As you begin today to build together a successful marriage you must choose who you will listen to — the wisdom of the world, or the word of God.

The wisdom of the world tells us that to be successful you have to put yourself first. The word of God in our lesson tells us that to be successful we must never put ourselves ahead of any other person. "Live in harmony" Paul writes (Romans 12:16). It may be that two people, each putting themselves first, are going to be successful in the world. I doubt they are going to be successful in their marriage.

Julie and John*, you have listened to the word of God on your wedding day, listen to those same words through all the days and weeks, months and years, of your married life. "Live in harmony with one another" (Romans 12:16). "Love one another with mutual affection; outdo one another in showing honor" (Romans 12:10). Each of you must find your own happiness in those things that make your partner happy. Never be so taken up with yourself that you ignore what is taking place in the heart and soul of your partner. Share each other's sorrows and joys. Those are the kinds of things that will make a successful marriage. If, together, you have a successful marriage, you each will have a successful life.

The wisdom of the world tells us that if we want to be successful, we can't be concerned about right or wrong. The only things that matter are the things that help us, and the things that hurt us, as we climb the ladder to the top. The word of God tells us that there are things that are right, and there are things that are wrong. "Hate what is evil, hold fast to what is good," writes Paul (Romans 12:9). It may be that two people, whose only concern is doing what it takes to climb the ladder, may be successful in the world but not in their marriage.

Julie and John*, you have listened to the word of God on your wedding day. Live your married life close to God and God will help you understand "what is good and acceptable and perfect" (Romans 12:2). Share the abilities you have been given, the money you will make, your love, your encouragement, your forgiveness, and offer your blessing. This world has so much need for good people like you doing good things. God's word is telling you that those things are the right things to do. When doing those things that are good and right is a priority for both of you, you will have a successful marriage. Having a successful marriage means that each of you will have a successful life.

The world thinks it knows what people need to do to have a successful life. Unfortunately the world is not so sure about what people need to do to have a successful marriage. God's word, the words we have listened to today, tell us how we can have both. May our couple*, may all the married couples here at this wedding, make the choice to live their lives together listening to the word of God. Listening to God can do so much to help us have successful marriages. Those who are married know that when you have a successful marriage, you also have a successful life.

Amen.

Be Transformed
Romans 12:1-18

"Conform." "Transform." These two words seem to bounce around everywhere in human history. Sometimes in our history, life is all about conforming, people joining together in some common way for some common purpose. Instead of individuals doing whatever they want, individuals adjust their own behavior and conform to what the community wants. At other times in history individuals take the initiative to change things. Instead of wanting things to be the way they always were, people act to change the world and transform what is into being something else, something new.

Conformity is not necessarily a bad thing. If everyone ran around trying to change things all the time, God's world would be a wilder and crazier place than most of us would find comfortable. Still there are dangers in conforming, dangers to our lives in marriage, and dangers to our living as God's people.

When what the people around us want most is getting as much as they can for themselves, conforming to that way of thinking is dangerous to marriage and dangerous to our living as children of God. When anything goes in how other people are treated, when people can be used and manipulated so long as we get what we want, conforming to that behavior is dangerous to marriage and dangerous to our living as God's children. We live in a world where a lot of things are disposable, but when relationships become included on the list of disposable items, conforming to that world is dangerous to marriage and dangerous to our living as children of God.

John and Julie*, in the scripture lesson from the twelfth chapter of Paul's letter to the Romans, the apostle presents each of us with a choice. We can either allow ourselves to "be conformed to this world," or we can "be transformed by the renewing of [our] minds, so that [we] may discern what is the will of God — what is good and acceptable and perfect" (Romans 12:2).

In a world littered with the remains of broken marriages, in a world where promises, along with faith and faithfulness, have become disposable, our God is not a God who conforms. Our God is a God who transforms. Our God is a God who makes us different from the world around us. God makes it possible for us to see life in a new way so that we become people who keep our promises, the promises we make in marriage and family, the promises we make to him, the promises we make to ourselves as his child, and the promises we make to others. Transformed people are people who make good promises and keep them.

Transformed people are people who see their partners in marriage, children, neighbors, the whole human family the same way God sees us. God sees everyone as people who are to be loved, not just sometime, but all the time; as people who are to be helped, not just when it is easy to do that but when helping hurts and when helping costs; as people who need to be accepted as we are, forgiven when we do wrong and given the encouragement we need to live our lives God's way.

John and Julie*, think how important it is because God sees you that way and treats you that way. The Apostle Paul wants you to know how important it is in your marriage and in your life when you see and treat each other and other people that same way, with constant love, with an ever-helping hand and an always attentive ear. As God accepts you as you are, forgives you, and encourages you, so be ready to accept, willing to forgive, and eager to encourage each other and all others.

As you begin your life together in marriage, don't allow yourselves to be conformed to the world, but allow God to continue his transforming work in your lives and in your marriage. Live close to God's word. Live close to Christ's church. Live close to God as you live close to each other. God's renewing presence will make a real difference in your marriage, and through your marriage, a real and important difference in his world.

Amen.

What Marriage Is
Romans 12; Philippians 4:8-9

One of the shocking discoveries we make in life is that this world is full of things that no one can identify. What is worse is that even the experts don't know. For me, it turns out that a lot of those things are under the hood of my car. I remember pointing out something to a mechanic. The conversation went as follows:
"What is that?"
"I don't know."
"What does it do?"
"It's got something to do with the emissions system."
"Does it work?"
"I don't know."
"What do I do if it doesn't work?"
"Get a new one."

When that happens it is best to close the hood, get in the car, crank up the car radio, and hope for the best, because if something doesn't work, and you don't know what it is, it's best not to think about it.

Another thing people don't seem to know how to clarify, is marriage.
"What is marriage?"
"I don't know."
"What's it about?"
"Something to do with love, having kids, and doing stuff together."
"What happens if it doesn't work?"
"Get a new one."

It's not so important for me or my mechanic to know what everything is under the hood of my car. Replacing something that has to do with emission control is no great tragedy, but divorce is. It is important for husbands and wives to know what marriage is so that if it isn't working, it can be repaired instead of junked.

Marriage is a way of living. Marriage is a lot of other things as well, but what it is in our world is a way of living. Marriage is a way of living with one, special other person. Marriage is a way in which those two people live together in the world.

In the scripture lessons read a few moments ago a way of living is laid out for people who want to live well. Those lessons speak to us today about a way of living for people who want to live well in marriage. It is a way of living that operates by love, kindness, respect, caring, sharing, forgiveness, patience, giving, humility, and being an emotional, as well as a physical, companion with another.

Marriage is a way of living that operates with kindness, faithfulness, and a willingness to draw upon the blessing and support of God. When two people live in marriage the way God intends people in marriage to live, good, lovely, and wonderful things take place in their lives and in the lives of those around them.

Marriage is a way of living. When it brings God's intended goodness to the relationship, we know that the way of living is working as it should.

When that way of living isn't working as it should, when goodness is not happening in the relationship, we don't have to junk the marriage. Since we know the way of living in marriage is all about those things spoken of in our scripture lessons, we know what it takes to get that way of living working. It takes love, kindness, respect, giving, caring, sharing, forgiveness, patience, humility, gentleness, and faithfulness.

Those are the things we need to fix our way of living in marriage so that it produces the goodness God intends marriages to have. Marriages are fixable, because our way of living in marriage is fixable. God will always be there to help us do what needs to be done in our living so that the goodness God wants marriages to have will continue to happen for husbands and wives.

John and Julie*, marriage is not only a way of living, it is your way of living, beginning today and in all the days, weeks, months, and years to come. Live in your marriage with love for each other with patience, forgiveness, humility, respect, kindness, gentleness, and caring. When that is the way the two of you live in your marriage, goodness will happen for you both. Should the day ever come when goodness isn't happening, don't give up on your life together. Fix your way of living with love, and all those other good things, and the goodness in your marriage will happen again.

    Amen.

Without Love I Am Nothing
1 Corinthians 13

"[If I] do not have love, I am nothing" (1 Corinthians 13:2). That's what the Apostle Paul wrote to the members of Christ's church in Corinth, "[If I] do not have love, I am nothing."

Like many people who are pastors in Christ's church, I was raised on Bible stories. I remember them all. I remember Adam and Eve in the garden, and I remember their son Abel and how he was murdered by his brother Cain. I remember Abraham and Sarah, and how Sarah had a baby when she was ninety years old. I remember Moses face-to-face with Pharaoh, commanding him in the name of God to, "Let my people go." I remember the Bible's super hero, long-haired Samson, fighting the whole Philistine army with only a piece of bone for a club. I remember young David in battle with the giant Goliath. I remember Daniel thrown into the lion's den. I remember Shadrach, Meshach, and Abednego strolling, unsinged, in the blazing fire of Nebuchadnezzar's furnace.

Of course I remember Mary and Joseph and how there was no room for them in the inn. I remember John the Baptist with his camel-skin clothes and his diet of grasshoppers and wild honey. I remember a disciple known as "Doubting Thomas," and a deacon named Stephen who did not doubt, but believed, and died for his faith.

I remember all those folks. I remember all the things the Bible said about them; their faith, their strength, and their courage. Funny thing, though. I don't remember the Bible ever saying anything about their love. Maybe their love was a given. Maybe it was just understood that love was the most important part of the life of every single one of those people. Maybe people who read the Bible are expected to know that each of the people whose stories I remember had a great love for God and each of them had a great love for other people.

They must have, because in his letter to the Corinthians the Apostle Paul tells us that without love, people are nothing. Those folks I mentioned certainly were not "nothing." The author of the biblical book of Hebrews speaks of those people as the great "cloud of witnesses" (Hebrews 12:1), which surrounds you and me and inspires us in our living as God's people.

Abraham wasn't the perfect husband to Sarah. Like all husbands, Abraham had his faults. But how he loved his wife. The Bible doesn't mention it, but of course he must have loved Sarah. If he hadn't, he would have been nothing and no one could ever call Abraham nothing. So added to the faith and faithfulness, for which Abraham is celebrated across the world, Abraham had to have a love that matched it.

Sarah was not a perfect wife to Abraham. Like every wife, Sarah had her faults. But how she loved her husband. The Bible doesn't mention it, but of course she must have loved Abraham, because without love, Sarah, the mother of nations would have been nothing. That could never be.

The Bible doesn't tell us about the love that was so much a part of the marriage of Abraham and Sarah. Maybe because that's something people are just supposed to know. It is understood that love was at the center of their marriage, love that was rich and powerful, love that was wonderful and miraculous, as real love always is. Such love had to have been there, because without it the marriage of Sarah and Abraham would have been nothing, instead of being one of the greatest relationships in all of human history.

Can you image the love that must have been in the marriage of Joseph and Mary? The Bible doesn't say a word about it. It doesn't have to, because without love Mary and Joseph would have been nothing. Their marriage would have been nothing. I think Jesus would have a lot to say about anyone daring to call his mother and his stepfather nothing.

These two people* haven't gotten to be a Bible story. Not yet, anyway. But they are great people, each of them, and this is a great marriage. What makes the two of them* great, what makes their marriage great, is their love. We know that because the Apostle Paul has told us what each of them would be without love. The Apostle Paul has told us what their marriage would be without love. This is

111

not a "nothing" day. This wedding day is a great day, a great day for two great people and their great marriage.

Today we celebrate the great things we know about these two people*. We celebrate the great things we know about their life together. As the Apostle Paul tells us, the greatest thing about them and their marriage is love. Love that is the gift of the Spirit. Love for God. Love for one another. Love for all of you here. Love for a whole world of people out there.

The two of you* keep in mind what the Apostle Paul writes about love. The best of who you are, the best of what your marriage is, comes from the love God has given to you and to your marriage. Because of that love, the two of you are "really something"! Because of that love your marriage will always be "really something"!

Amen.

The Greater Gift
1 Corinthians 12:31—13:8; 1 John 3:18-24

I had intended to use this time in the wedding to narrate the creation story in Genesis 2, with the bride and groom* acting out the roles of Adam and Eve. I think you would have enjoyed it, and it would have saved the bride and groom* a bundle on wedding clothes. Trouble was, I didn't tell them about it soon enough. By then the bride* had bought her dress and the groom* had rented his tux. What this means is that you folks here will be blessed with a sermon, just as, for the rest of their lives, the bride and groom* will be blessed with each other.

Now a really good sermon can be a joy to listen to. So, too, a really good marriage can be a joy to experience. I can't say that this is a really good sermon. What I can say is that it will be short. What I can say about the marriage of these two people* is what you already know. They have a really good relationship. While my sermon might be short, I believe and hope that their life together will be long and happy.

The reason I know that our bride and groom* have such a good relationship is because of the scripture lessons they have included in their wedding service. Both lessons are about love.

Our lesson in 1 John is about God's love for us, love that shined its brightest in God's gift of his Son to us. In Jesus we experience a love for us that is so deep that God was willing to give his Son, and Jesus was willing to give his own life, so that you and I might not die but live in him and with him forever.

Our bride and groom* have anchored their lives, and their marriage, in God's love. The strong foundation of their life together rests upon the love of God, and all God's gifts for living that are coming to them because of that love. Any relationship founded on God's love is a good relationship. That's how I know this marriage is a really good marriage.

The second of our two scripture lessons is about the love God gives us to use in our lives together. In Paul's first letter to the Corinthians we are shown what this love looks like. It is love that looks like patience. It is love that looks like kindness. It is love that looks like humility. It is love that looks like one person listening deeply to another. It is love that looks like one person speaking softy to another. It is love that looks like one person enthusiastically celebrating the other. It is love that looks like one person forgiving another without limit. It is love that looks like a mindset that forgets every bad day and treasures the memory of every good day.

Any relationship in which love looks like the love described in our scripture lesson is a good relationship. Because our bride and groom* want the love in their marriage to have that look to it, their marriage is a really good marriage.

First Corinthians 13 is read at a lot of weddings. What is not often read is the scripture verse that precedes it in chapter 12, "Strive for the greater gifts... [the] excellent way" (1 Corinthians 12:31 NRSV).

The best love, the most excellent love, is the love we receive as a gift from God. This love is manufactured within us by the living presence of Jesus Christ, brought to us by God's Holy Spirit. No love of our own can match the love that we receive as a gift of God. Any relationship is a good relationship when the love within that relationship is continually received and renewed through the inner working of the greatest lover humankind has ever known.

Because our bride and groom* have opened their lives to this gift of love, alive and at work within them, their marriage has everything it needs to be really good.

The sermon is over, short and sweet, I hope. The marriage of our bride and groom* is beginning, long and happy, I pray.

Amen.

Registered With God
1 Corinthians 13; 1 John 4:7-12

Let's talk wedding gifts. John and Julie*, what do you think will be the best wedding gift you are going to be given? A wide-slot toaster has to be near the top of the list. A bread machine would be terrific, unless both of you are on one of those low-carb diets. Wouldn't it be nice if, in one of your cards there are two tickets for a Caribbean cruise?

Myself, I like weddings where the couple is registered at Goodwill. Gifts might not be fancy, but you get value for the money and that's important. I am glad to see where the two of you did register. I don't mean Goodwill or some other store. I'm glad you registered with God. You probably don't remember doing that, but your parents do. They brought you to worship, held you over the baptism font, and the pastor poured water over your head. With the splashing of that water, in the name of the Father, the Son, and the Holy Spirit, each of you were registered forever with God.

Being registered with God is the best thing that is ever going to happen to you. It has a special goodness for today. That's because that's where your best wedding gift is coming from. It's going to come from God. God's Son, Jesus, bought it for you. Together, Father and Son sent the Holy Spirit to bring it to your wedding. The gift is love.

As the Apostle Paul writes in the thirteenth chapter of his first letter to the Corinthians, God has some great wedding gifts for you. Faith is one of them. "Letting go, and letting God," can take a lot of worry and anxiety out of married life. "Cast all your anxiety on [God], because he cares for you" (1 Peter 5:7 NRSV). That's what the gift of faith enables husbands and wives to do. By doing that, marriage and family life is a whole lot happier.

Faith is one of the wedding gifts God is giving you. Hope is another. Hope has to be one of God's best wedding gifts. Every wedding day is a day of hope, your hopes for your future together, and our hopes for your future together. At weddings, hope floats up like the bubbles of a champagne toast. Among those hopes there is one that lasts forever. The hope you receive as a gift of God.

Faith and hope are gifts God is giving to the two of you on your wedding day. They are both great gifts because, as Paul writes, neither of them will ever wear out.

But God has one more wedding gift for you. According to Paul, it is the best gift of all. That gift is love.

God's gift of love is yours. It is yours to use in your marriage. Like faith and hope, it will never wear out. You can use it every day. Each morning, when you wash your face, the Holy Spirit will be there in that water renewing God's gift of love, the gift you registered for in the water of your baptism.

I hate to say this in front of your guests, but some of the gifts they are giving you today will never be used. That battery-powered garlic press will stay in its box forever. I guess that's okay for a gift like that, but don't let the same thing happen to the gifts you are given by God: faith, hope, love. You got 'em. So, use 'em.

Amen.

God Is Love
(Apple Orchard Wedding)
1 Corinthians 13; 1 John 4:16

What is more beautiful than an orchard in blossom? What is sweeter than an apple pie with sugar sprinkled on the crust? What is warmer than summer sunshine? What is more tender than a tear in the eye of a bride on her wedding day? What is stronger than the wind that ushers in a springtime storm? Let me give you a hint. It was mentioned nine times in the scripture lesson that has just been read. You guessed it, it is love, beautiful, sweet, warm, tender, and, most of all, strong.

According to God's word, love is the most powerful force in the universe. There is more power in love than in all the power of all the weapons, in all the armies, in all the world. The Bible never says, God is military might, but the Bible does say, "God is love" (1 John 4:16).

There is more power in love than in all the economic power, in all the money, in all the vaults, in all the banks, in all the world. The Bible never says, God is wealth, but the Bible does say, "God is love" (1 John 4:16).

There is more power in love than in all the stubborn strength of all the self-willed, self-centered, people in all the homes, in all the lands, in all the world. The Bible never says, God is having your own way, but the Bible does say, "God is love" (1 John 4:16).

There is more power in love than in all collected energy of all the happiness that can be achieved by all the people who are pursuing their own happiness in every place, every way, everywhere in the world. The Bible never says God is happiness, but the Bible does say, "God is love" (1 John 4:16).

The generals and their armies have had their chance to make this world a better place. They haven't done it. Money has had its chance to bring human living to new levels of goodness. Good things have happened when money is used for good purposes, but in many ways, the more things have changed, the more they have stayed the same. Self-centeredness has only made things worse. The pursuit of happiness has led to a dead end.

Isn't it time that love has its turn? Isn't it time for love to show what it can do in our world, our families, and our marriages? We need to give love a chance. We need to give the love we see in Jesus a chance in the way each person lives their lives. We need to give the love described in our lesson by the Apostle Paul a chance in the way each person lives their lives. The world has given everything else a chance. It is time for the world to give love a chance.

Maybe there isn't much most of us can do to make the whole world do that, but there is a lot each of us can do to make ourselves do that. Our bride and groom*, will you do that? Will you give love a chance to show what it can do in your life together? Love has the power to do wonderful things, because God has the power to do wonderful things and, "God is love" (1 John 4:16).

The power in love can make your marriage blossom with more beauty than an apple orchard in springtime. The power in love can make your life together sweeter than an apple pie with sugar sprinkled on the crust. The power in love can make your companionship warmer than summer sunshine. The power in love can give this new life of yours a tenderness that will bring tears to the eyes of all those who celebrate its beginning here with you today. The power in love can protect you though the worst of any storms the world blows into your marriage. Remember, "God is love" (1 John 4:16). There is no end to what God, and love, can do when you give it a chance in the new "apple orchard" life the two of you are beginning, together, today.

Amen.

Get Ready to Fight
1 Corinthians 16:13-14

"Keep alert, stand firm in your faith, be courageous, be strong" (1 Corinthians 16:13).

These words don't sound like the two of you are being sent into life together as husband and wife. These words sound like the two of you are being sent into battle. Maybe you are. Maybe marriage, the kind of marriage God wants the two of you to have, involves a battle. Maybe all of life, the kind of life God wants us each to live, involves a battle.

That's the way the Apostle Paul saw it. Paul understood that there is an enemy at work in this world — an enemy of God and an enemy of human life and human goodness. The work this enemy seeks to do is to separate people from God, separate people from each other, and, one by one, take away from us that precious goodness our loving God has given to our lives.

Therefore, Paul warns us to "keep alert." The enemy is out there in the world around us, and the enemy is here, in the world within us. We each must be prepared to do battle in defense of everything that is good in our lives, and in the lives of those who share our living with us.

For husbands and wives marriage is a battle, a fight. It is not a fight against each other, it is a fight for each other, for the goodness of their life together. Husbands and wives must stand side by side, courageous and strong in defense of everything that is good and God-pleasing in their marriage, family, and the world in which they live.

Today the two of you* are making promises to each other, promises of support, encouragement, love and faithfulness, and understanding and mutual respect. You are promising to defend each other and your marriage against any and every enemy.

Paul wants you to know that there is an enemy out there. This enemy is going to try to make you forget the promises you make today. This enemy is going to try to make you lose faith in the goodness of your marriage. This enemy is going to try to make you lose faith in God. This enemy is going to try to make you lose faith in the help God is giving each of you to make and keep your marriage the good thing God intends it to be.

"Keep alert, stand firm in your faith, be courageous, be strong" (1 Corinthians 16:13). Most of all, "Let all that you do be done in love" (1 Corinthians 16:14). Your marriage has the blessing and the support of God. God, who does everything in love, is with you, fighting for the goodness of your life together. Through Jesus, God shows you how to bring goodness to each other and to those who share your living with you. Through the Holy Spirit, God gives each of you the tools you need to have a good marriage.

The two of you* must keep the faith. Keep that faith. Stand together, strong and courageous. Don't be afraid to fight. Fight for the goodness of your marriage. "Let all you do be done in love," and you cannot lose.

Amen.

Real Love and Real Life
1 Corinthians 13; Romans 12:9-18

There are two themes intertwined in the scripture lessons our couple* has included in their wedding. The two themes are love and life. God's word teaches us how we are to love each other, and God's word teaches us how we are to live with each other. Marriage is, of course, about both. Marriage is about loving and about living.

As Paul reminds the Corinthians in that wonderful thirteenth chapter of his first letter, life in the church is a disaster when it is lived without love. The same is true of life in marriage. Married life is a disaster when it is lived without love. Big bank accounts, nice homes, vacations in the Bahamas, successful careers, but none of those things can give marriage the goodness God intends marriage to have. Only love can do that. Without love, married life cannot prosper, even though it might have everything else. With love, the kind of love Paul describes to the Corinthians, the kind of love our Lord exemplified in all his words and deeds, married life will prosper. If it has love, married life will prosper, even though that life might not have much of anything else.

So, too, family life is a disaster without love, without love's patience and kindness. When family life does not have love, it is headed for disaster, because God's gift of love is the only antidote for those things that make life together painful and tearful: jealousies, conceits, pride, selfishness, irritability. Family life may have many good things about it, but the one thing that is indispensable for family life is love.

By including the thirteenth chapter of Paul's first letter to the Corinthians in their wedding, our couple* has shown that they want today to be about love. By including the verses from the twelfth chapter of Paul's letter to the Romans, they have shown that they want today to be about life.

As our Lord Jesus has shown the human race so clearly, real love is about real living. There is more to marriage than Valentine's Day sentiment and gifts on anniversaries. There is daily living, money to earn and bills to pay, grass to cut and meals to fix. There are mistakes to forgive and quarrels to resolve. There are choices to make and obligations to meet. There are tugs pulling this way and that. There are temptations to overcome. Married life is real living, just as family life is real living. To pretend otherwise, to believe there is no hard work and no problems in married and family life, is to live in a house built of cards that will crash down at the first gust of wind.

We need to know how to love together in marriage and family, and we need to know how to live together in marriage and family. God's word, directing our attention to Jesus, helps us to do both, bring real loving to real living. Following the example of our Lord we put love to work in the service of life forgiving one another as he forgives us. Opening our arms to one another, as he opens his arms to us. Drying one another's tears, as Jesus so often dries our tears. Listening to others, as our Lord Jesus so patiently listens to us. Encouraging the best from one another, as Jesus encourages the best from us. Helping to carry one another's burdens, as Jesus helps us carry ours. Bringing one another in prayer to God, as Jesus brings us to his heavenly Father in prayer. All those things are real love at work in real life.

Jesus shows us how real love works in the service of real life. Jesus also shows us how real life works in the service of real love. At the table; on the road; fishing on the lake; preaching on a hilltop or a wedding or a funeral; with family, friends, in a crowd, in the morning hours and after a long day's work; wherever he was in real life, Jesus acted with real love. There were not just some occasions when Jesus showed that love is possible. Jesus showed us that in every occasion in life, love is possible. That was true in his life with us. He wants us to know that it is true in our life with each other in our communities, our marriages, and our families. In every occasion in real life, it is possible for each of us to act with real love.

John and Julie* the scripture lessons read today have been about love and about life. You have included them in your wedding, now include them in your love together, and include them in your life together. These words from the Bible point you to Jesus. It is Jesus who will show you how to put real love to work in your real life, in your marriage and in your family. It is Jesus who will show you how your real life, in your marriage and in your family, is where your real love must do its work.

Amen.

Love or Nothing
1 Corinthians 13

The thirteenth chapter of the Apostle Paul's first letter to the Corinthians makes it clear that Paul had a thing about love. Paul expected love to perform miracles. You know what? He was right.

It was God's love in Jesus Christ that accomplished the miracle that is our salvation. It was love that did it. "For God so loved the world that he gave his only Son" (John 3:16).

It was Jesus' love that created the miracle that is his church. "As the Father has loved me," Jesus said, "so I have loved you" (John 15:9). In that love, Jesus' love for those he died on the cross to save, the church — his church, was born.

Love, as our Lord commanded us to love, love his way, love Jesus' way, accomplishes the miracle of a whole new way for human beings to live. "Love your enemies," Jesus says (Matthew 5:44). Christians don't always do that, to our shame, and to the world's loss. But when we do, when we love as Jesus loves, when we love not only our friends but also our enemies, it is a miracle. It is a miracle that takes the world by surprise. It is love that does it. The miracle happens because God's love is at work in us making the impossible possible.

As everyone who has ever stood before God and exchanged wedding promises knows, marriage is a miracle. Two people becoming one, that's a miracle, and it is love that makes that miracle happen. These two people being married today* are being transformed, transformed from something each of them has always been into something new that the two of them together are becoming. That radical transformation of human nature is a miracle. None of their teachers in school taught them how to make that happen. No self-help book they could buy from a bookstore could tell them how to do it. They couldn't learn it from Oprah Winfrey or Dr. Phil. The miracle that is at work in these two people* is happening because of love. The love their Creator God has for them has provided these two people*, as it provided Adam and Eve, the perfect opportunity for them to love each other.

The love God has for them has gifted each of them* with the Holy Spirit's gift of love, love as it is wonderfully described in 1 Corinthians 13. Love that is patient and kind. Love that builds up and encourages, love that forgives and understands, love that holds tightly to what is good and what is true. That love is a miracle, and the miracle taking place in these two people* and their life together is nourished by that love.

The two of you*, never forget the miracles that love has already accomplished in bringing you together and bringing you here. Leave here knowing that there is nothing love cannot accomplish in your life together. The miracles that love, God's love, your love, can bring about in your lives have just begun. There are many things necessary to make marriage and family life work, but the thing that does the miracles is love.

Amen.

The Frontier
(Cowboy Wedding)
1 Corinthians 13:4-13; 1 John 4:14-21

I think it is fair to say the neither the Apostle Paul, the disciple John, nor the Lord himself could be described as a cowboy. As far as I know none of them ever used "howdy pardner" as a greeting. Nothing in the New Testament suggests that any of them ever wore spurs that "jingle, jangle, jingle." To them the Old West was anything on the other side of Athens, Greece.

They were easterners, our Lord, John, and Paul. More specifically, they were middle-easterners, but they weren't dudes. Remember that. Paul, John, and Jesus were not dudes. They were frontiersmen. They deserve the deepest respect from every man and woman who has ever tied their horses together at the hitching post of life. Marriage today is life on the frontier. Married couples have a lot to learn from those three trailblazers: Paul, John, and Jesus of Nazareth.

The frontier is a place without rules, a place where it is every person for themselves. That's kind of where marriage is today. The old rules are gone. Husbands and wives are left on their own to look after their own survival; to lasso, hog-tie, and brand their own personal happiness.

The frontier is a wide-open place with all sorts of wonders to discover and all sorts of dangers to avoid. That might not be the best description of marriage, but it will do.

God's word in the New Testament is a guide to life on the frontier, living where the old rules no longer apply. What Jesus, John, and Paul are telling us is that the most important thing frontiersmen and frontierswomen need to know is how to love.

What is going to make this frontier marriage work is not that these two people* are good with their guns. What is going to make this frontier marriage work is that these two people* are good with their hearts, and they can put the instructions of our Lord, Paul, and John into practice in their life together.

To make their marriage work on the frontier these two people* are going to have to love each other the way God loves them. They are going to have to love each other with a love that never stops giving and a love that never stops forgiving. In a world where a lot of marriage spreads are busting up, these two people* are going to have to love each other with a love that is always ready to listen, understand, and respond with a kindness and a gentleness that encourages, comforts, strengthens, directs, even corrects, in ways that build up their life together.

When we enter the frontier, it helps to have someone we can trust riding ahead to blaze a trail for us. Jesus, Paul, and John do that. They are out there in a life where the old rules have been left behind. They are out there showing us the trail. The trail they set is love, living within God's love and living by loving each other. Remember that as the two of you* saddle up and ride off into the sunset together.

Amen.

The Garden of Eden
(Outdoor Wedding)
1 Corinthians 13:1-7

John and Julie*, I've some good news and some bad news for you on your wedding day. First the bad news. As far as I can tell, as beautiful as this place is, it is not the Garden of Eden. Sure it's pretty, but the geography is all wrong. We are told in Genesis 2 that there were four rivers in the Garden of Eden. Unfortunately, none of the rivers close to us are mentioned as being any of them.

The good news is that the scripture text you have included in your wedding gives you a Garden of Eden way to live your married life. In Genesis 2, the Bible tells us the Garden of Eden was the perfect place to live. In 1 Corinthians 13, the Bible tells us the perfect way to live. That way is love.

Garden of Eden love is not just any kind of love. Garden of Eden love looks like Jesus, the greatest lover the planet earth has ever known. Garden of Eden love is love that never stops giving. Garden of Eden love is love that never stops forgiving. Garden of Eden love is love that has the ability to see the other person's need and the focus and determination to meet that need.

Garden of Eden love is love that is always willing to listen, always willing to understand, always willing to respond with kindness, gentleness, and humility. Garden of Eden love is love that even when it disagrees with another person, it does so in ways that build the other person up instead of tearing them down. Garden of Eden love is love that uses the whole body in its service, heart and hands, mouth and ears.

Garden of Eden love is perfect love. Our Lord Jesus was able to use that love perfectly, sacrificing his life for our lives, going to the cross for our salvation.

I don't suppose I have to tell you that you are not Jesus. That's more bad news. But there is more good news too. Jesus is with you. In your baptism Jesus has made himself part of your life. In your baptism Jesus has made you as part of his life. The good news is that Jesus will help you live Garden of Eden love in his own perfect way.

John and Julie*, let Jesus do that. Open your married life to him in prayer and worship. You are going to spend your married life together in a world that is not the Garden of Eden. Let Jesus give you the help you need. Let Jesus give your love the help it needs for the two of you to live in the not-Eden world as Garden-of-Eden people and striving always for perfection in your love for each other.

Amen.

Marvelous Words for Marriage
1 Corinthians 13; Philippians 4:4-9

John and Julie*, there are some marvelous words for marriage in the scripture lessons being read at your wedding. First, there is the word "love." The Apostle Paul repeats that word over and over again in the thirteenth chapter of his letter to the church in Corinth. Love, without which anything we are or do comes to nothing. That is true in our living in the world. It is even truer in our life together in marriage. Without love at its heart and soul, a marriage is poor indeed, with a poverty far more serious than a simple shortage of money.

As he describes love at work, Paul uses other marvelous words for marriage.

Patience: A willingness to put a bridle on our fussy restlessness over another person's behavior.

Kindness: So simple a word, so important an action in relationships, so profoundly important in the way husbands and wives relate to one another in marriage. Kindness present is a cause for grateful smiles, and kindness absent releases a fountain of tears.

Truth: People can maintain some relationships by pretending, by hiding true feelings, by adopting artificial behavior. People can do that in some relationships, but it can't be done in the relationship in marriage. In marriage the truth about us cannot be hidden. That truth may not always be attractive, but if it is grounded in mutual love, it will not destroy a marriage. Instead it will enrich the understanding and acceptance that is love at work.

In his letter to the church in Philippi, the Apostle Paul includes more marvelous words for marriage.

Joy: The joy in marriage is not an absence of sorrow. No marriage and no family is without sorrow. There are losses. There are partings. There is pain we cause one another because we are not perfect. Joy in marriage is that unbreakable sense of goodness in this relationship God has given. That deep joy keeps married couples together and carries them through the times of sorrow. Joy in marriage is not simply delight in the present, it is hope for the future. It is anchored in promises made, believed, and kept.

Thankfulness: People don't always express their thankfulness in marriage. Husbands and wives allow each other to take much of what they do for granted. That, of course, shouldn't stop us from saying "thank you" as often as we can. Still the real thankfulness in marriage is a deeper thing. It is a mutual sense of gratitude, a grateful spirit, sensed and shared in each other. It is a thankfulness ultimately directed toward God, who gives us to each other and who gives us all the good that is ours in life and in marriage.

Peace: Peace that is alive and vital. Peace that is not simply the absence of hostility, but a reaching out to one another in marriage, creating a mutual understanding that calms restless spirits and eases troubled minds.

Gentleness: "Let your gentleness be known to everyone" (Philippians 4:5), writes Paul. In his letter to the Galatians, Paul identifies gentleness as one of the fruits of the Holy Spirit. Blessed is the marriage where such good fruit grows in abundance.

John and Julie*, God is giving you marvelous words for your wedding day and marvelous words for your marriage. With so much going on for you, today is not the best day for listening. Tomorrow will be better. May God grant you countless tomorrows of listening to him and bringing his words to life in your marriage. May love, patience, kindness, truth, joy, thankfulness, peace, and gentleness describe not only words the two of you are hearing, but the life the two of you are living. Today God is giving you these marvelous words and may they help you have a marvelous marriage.

Amen.

Love: Before and After
1 Corinthians 13

Better preachers than I have delivered marvelous wedding sermons about the many kinds of love in marriage. I suspect they have more poetic souls than I do. In my unimaginative understanding I can see only two kinds of love in marriage: love before the wedding day and love after the wedding day. As many of the married guests will tell you, the two loves are not the same.

Love before the wedding day is full of wonderful generalities of always and forever. Love before the wedding day is songs that melt the heart and moisten the eye. Love before the wedding day is a thing of hopes and dreams and special times together in a world almost more than real. Love before the wedding day is wonderfully blind to everything except what it wants to see. Love before the wedding day sees the future for what it could be.

Love after the wedding day isn't much about generalities. It is much more about specifics. Love after the wedding day is very much about the now, and not much about the forever. Love after the wedding day is not songs sung, but words spoken and things done. Love after the wedding day is living in the real world spending all times together, not just spending some special times together. Love after the wedding day is not about two people hoping. It is about two people helping. Love after the wedding day is sharp eyed, seeing everything, even things it would rather not see. Love after the wedding day knows the present for what it is, and love after the wedding day knows the future for where the present is taking it.

Two kinds of love in marriage. Love before the wedding day and love after the wedding day. The sad truth too often is that the one does not lead into the other. Love before the wedding, with all its generalities, sometimes cannot translate itself into love after the wedding day, love with all its specifics.

John and Julie*, in the thirteenth chapter of Paul's first letter to the Corinthians, read a few moments ago, the apostle is not writing about the love that brought you here today, love before the wedding. Paul is writing about your love after today, the love that belongs to the specifics of your life together, the love that belongs to all the mornings, afternoons, and evenings in all the years to come. Paul is writing about love that takes life together as it is, and expresses itself in that real life in real ways. Those real ways include being patient with each other; being kind to each other; trusting each other; understanding each other; accepting, forgiving, and looking after each other. Love after your wedding is love you show by your honesty and openness with each other, by your willingness to listen to each other, respect and value each other's opinions and points of view. The love the Apostle Paul writes about, your love for each other after your wedding, is love that never quits and never gives up.

John and Julie*, we know of the wonderful love for each other that brought you here today. Today is all about letting loose with your full-blown celebration of that love, and thanking God for bringing the two of you together. That love tells the story of your wedding, but the love you give to each other after today will tell the story of your marriage. God will be generous in giving you everything you need to live out his gift of love in your life together. As God is generous in giving it, be generous in using it. May your love after your wedding day be even stronger and more beautiful than the love that is giving such beauty to today.

Amen.

Perfect Love
1 Corinthians 13

Love is a wonderful thing. Listen again to what the Apostle Paul is saying about it. "Love is patient; love is kind; love is not envious or boastful or arrogant or rude. [Love] does not insist on its own way, it is not irritable or resentful. [Love] does not rejoice in wrongdoing, but rejoices in the truth. [Love] bears all things, believes all things, hopes all things, endures all things" (1 Corinthians 13:4-7).

Love is just about perfect. Too bad people aren't. People can be, and often are, impatient and unkind. People can be, and often are, envious, boastful, arrogant, and rude. People often do insist on their own way. We can be irritable and resentful. Oh, how happy we are when someone who has given us trouble has trouble themselves. Love may never give up, but people do. Our faith in another person can collapse. Our hopes for a relationship can be abandoned. There are times we give up on each other way too easily.

One of the problems that has plagued the human family is how to bring people and love together so that love can lend its perfection to imperfect people.

Romance can do that. Falling in love can bring two imperfect people together in a mysterious, almost magical relationship. For people in love, the emotional power of the good things cementing their relationship overwhelms the imperfections. Like blossoms in a flower garden, hiding the weeds growing beneath, romantic love keeps the bad things in the relationship from being seen. To romantic love everything is perfect, even imperfect people.

The trouble is like a blossom on a flower, romantic love doesn't last forever. The time comes when the weeds are no longer hidden. The time comes in our relationships when our imperfections become visible to each other. The problem remains. When the superheated emotions of romance begin to cool, how can love in its perfection be brought together with people in our imperfection?

The solution to the problem does not come from us. It comes from God. In Jesus Christ, God has brought the perfection of his love and the imperfection of people together for all eternity. What we are not, Jesus is for us; forgiver, healer, renewer, Savior. What we are not, Jesus enables us to be. Jesus inspires, and through the Holy Spirit enables, imperfect people to love with his love, to treat one another as Jesus treats us, with forgiveness, encouragement, acceptance, a listening ear, a caring heart, and a gentle, calming touch. Through Jesus, our imperfections do not prevent us from being good to each other, and for the sake of one another, building married life together in shapes and patterns of his goodness.

John and Julie*, I know you want what you have now in your relationship to last forever. To you and to us your love seems so good and perfect. Your task as husband and wife is to keep love's perfection stronger than your imperfection. In that task of building and living your life together, make use of the inner power Jesus shares with you in word and sacrament. Let Jesus inspire you and guide you as you live out a lifetime of love for one another, and a lifetime of love reaching out from you to the world.

Let Jesus be for you what you are not so that, should your own love stumble, Jesus' love will continue through you. Let Jesus enable you to be what you need to be for each other; patient and kind, always happy with each other's successes, and always willing to forgive each other's mistakes. Let Jesus enable you to have unlimited faith in one another, unlimited hope for what your life together will be, untiring energy to maintain all the goodness your love for each other has now, and unending commitment to use all the gifts Jesus is giving you to keep your love growing stronger and deeper in all the days, weeks, months, and years of your life together.

Don't worry about not being perfect. With the perfection of Jesus' love at work within you, the goodness of your marriage has everything it is ever going to need.

Amen.

The Look of Love
1 Corinthians 13

"Love" is a marvelous word. In the thirteen verses of our scripture lesson from 1 Corinthians the Apostle Paul uses the word love nine times. In the gospel of John, our Lord Jesus uses the word love more than two dozen times. Love is a marvelous word for us to hear. Love is also a beautiful thing for us to see.

Julie Alice Johnson* is in love. We see that love in the sparkle of her eyes. John David Clinton* is also in love. We see that love in the gentleness of his* touch as he holds Julie's* hand in his.

Love is a marvelous word. It conjures up so many images of life at its best. Love is a goodnight kiss. Love is a bouquet of flowers on Valentine's Day. Love is a whisper that brings a smile and a hug. Love is a new mother cradling her firstborn child in her arms.

Love is a man bleeding on a cross. That picture is not as pretty as the others. A man bleeding on a cross hardly seems the image of life at its best. Certainly the people who nailed that man to the cross were not living at their best. It was the man on the cross, it was Jesus, who was living at his best, living the best of love and laying down his life for another. Giving his life for us.

Love is a sparkle in the eyes. Love is a tender touch. Love is a goodnight kiss. Love is flowers and babies. Love is a man bleeding on a cross. Love is caring at the deepest level of the human heart. Love is giving, not just a little, but a lot. Love is giving without limit and whatever the cost. Love is being kind in a world that is often cruel. Love is helping others even when they are hurting you. Love is forgiving before anyone says, "I'm sorry."

Jesus knew how to love. Whenever we want to see what love looks like, all we have to do is look at Jesus. The life of Jesus has the look of love. When we see Jesus giving sight to the blind man, we see love. When we see Jesus feeding the hungry, we see love. When we see Jesus spending time with the children, we see love. When we see Jesus on his knees, washing his disciple's feet, we see love. Most of all, when we see Jesus dying on the cross to give new life to you and me, we see what real love looks like.

John and Julie*, when we look at the two of you, we see love. Give the look of love to your whole life together. In your marriage, paint love's pretty pictures, scenes of happiness, and delight. Also, let love be seen in your marriage in the not so pretty pictures, times of pain, work, and sacrifice. Whatever your marriage brings, show us what real love looks like.

When we read our Bibles, love is a marvelous word to hear. When we look at Jesus, love is a marvelous thing to see. John and Julie*, your wedding today has the look of love. May that also be true of your marriage. Learning from Jesus, give your whole life together the look of love.

Amen.

Marriage Is Giving
2 Corinthians 8:5

"They gave themselves first to the Lord" (2 Corinthians 8:5 NRSV). Those are the words of the Apostle Paul. They are also the word of God. "They gave themselves first to the Lord." For the two of you*, I hope that is where your giving begins, giving yourselves to the Lord, who gave himself for you.

Giving begins in God. God gives his Son to the world he loves. Jesus gives himself to the world of people he loves. Through the love the Holy Spirit gives birth to within us, we first give ourselves, through Jesus, to God. Then the giving that begins with God goes on in our lives to become the giving that goes into our marriages, the giving that goes into our families, the giving that goes into our communities, and the giving that goes out to our friends and neighbors. The giving that begins in God goes on through us to become the giving that carries out love's work and God's work, at home and around the world.

When the value of your life together is added up, its worth will not be measured in what you have. Its worth will be measured in how you gave. That's God's word to you on your wedding day.

I am sure the two of you have looked around and have seen a lot of people who have more money than you do, who have nicer homes than you do, who have newer cars, cabins at the lake, boats, and jet skies, SUVs, ATVs, and IRAs all from what is in their ATMs.

I don't have to tell you what you should do when you see all those people who have so much. You know yourselves that whining, complaining, and feeling sorry for yourselves is a waste of time. Instead you should do what the Apostle Paul says the Christians in Macedonia did. You should go right on giving yourselves to the Lord, giving yourselves in love to each other, giving yourselves in love to your family, and giving yourselves in friendship to all the people who have come to be with you today. Part of that giving will be prayers, your prayers. Part of that giving will be help, your help, your words and deeds, which give happiness and hope. Some of the people in the world who have the most, don't begin to give what the two of you have already been giving, and what the two of you will be giving in all the years of your life together.

"They gave themselves first to the Lord, and, by the will of God, to us" (2 Corinthians 8:5 NRSV). Our Lord informs us, through the Apostle Paul, that how much we give has nothing to do with how much we have. People who have a lot don't necessarily give a lot. People who have a little are not prevented from being generous in their giving by the little they have. That's the way it was for the faithful Christians in Macedonia. Paul tells us that they had very little but that did not stop them from giving a lot.

Too often when we think of giving, we think of money. That is part of what Paul was referring to when he writes about the Christians in Macedonia. They gave financial support to the mission work of spreading the gospel. But to that work they also would have given their hearts, prayers, encouragement, good words, and good deeds. Because you give yourselves first to the Lord, those are the things the two of you will always have to give to each other, your family, your friends, the world around you; prayers, heart-felt love, encouragement, good words, and good deeds.

For the two of you*, may these words of Paul, read at your wedding, be the story of your living as husband and wife, so that family, friends, and others can say about you, "They gave themselves first to the Lord, and, by the will of God, to each other and to us."

Amen.

Heart Work and Head Work
Galatians 5:22-23a; Romans 12:2

Marriage is a matter of the heart. It is from the deepest stirring of our hearts that the direction of this most special of relationships is established, moving our lives ever closer to each other.

Marriage is a matter of the heart. Unable to be content with the Adam-like loneliness that is so much a part of our being human, our hearts seek the companionship of others and the deeper companionship of that one special other in whose company our loneliness dissolves.

Marriage is a matter of the heart. Yet being married requires more that heart work. Being married is also head work. Our hearts contribute their share to the relationship. Our heads contribute their share as well. We share our thoughts about ourselves, life, and God. We learn new things about each other. We plan together and make decisions together. This head work is not a secondary thing to being married, not at all. Marriage is heart work. Being married is work that we do with our hearts and with our heads.

God knows that. He who established marriage in the Garden and continues to bless marriage in the world, sends his Holy Spirit to work in our hearts and in our heads. The Holy Spirit works in our hearts, gifting us with kindness and patience, humility and trust, and all those things needed so that we love one another as God loves us. The Holy Spirit works in our heads, giving us new ways of understanding God's will, and how we are to live as God's children in our life together in marriage.

Marriage is a matter of the heart. John and Julie*, your hearts have brought you to each other and here today. Marriage is a matter of the heart, being married is a matter of the heart and of the head. You have delightful hearts and capable heads, just the stuff from which a wonderful marriage can be built. Throughout your married life, open your hearts and your minds to God's Holy Spirit. Together live close to God's word and live close to Christ's church. The Holy Spirit at work in your hearts and in your heads will help make being married everything your God wants it to be. The Holy Spirit at work in your hearts and in your heads will help make being married everything you both want it to be.

Amen.

The Chicken or the Egg
Ephesians 5:21-33

"Wives, be subject to your husbands" (Ephesians 5:22). "Husbands, love your wives" (Ephesians 5:25).

Which comes first? This is no chicken or egg puzzle. The answer to this question is desperately important for every husband or wife who reads these words of the Apostle Paul.

Does the wife allow herself to be submissive to her husband, and so earn her husband's love? But what if he fails to respond in love? What if he ignores her or abuses her? What, then, has her submission earned for her? A pillow wet with tears, a black eye, a broken, sorrowful spirit. Those are the rewards of marriage for her.

Does the husband reach out first to his wife with love? Does his love for her give her the guarantee and assurance that by entrusting herself to him she will not be hurt, taken advantage of, or made miserable? Will she be comforted, treasured, rejoiced over and rejoiced with, set free to feel whole, and worthwhile as a person, wife, mother?

The Apostle Paul, in his words to the Ephesians, leaves no doubt about who does what first, the wife submitting or the husband loving. Paul writes about the relationship of husbands and wives being like the relationship of Jesus and the church. The church was born out of Jesus' love. Jesus' love created the church. Jesus' love undergirds the church. Jesus' love opens the future for the church.

Because its Lord is so completely full of love, the church can freely and joyfully entrust itself to him and be safe and secure. Jesus' love for his church does not put the church into a kind of submissive slavery. Jesus' love sets his church free to live out its life and carry out its mission.

"Wives, be subject to your husbands." "Husbands, love your wives." Which of these comes first? A husband's love, of course, first, last, and always. John*, you are to love Julie* without limit.

You are to love Julie* with no strings attached. You are to love Julie* with the same depth and faithfulness Jesus shows in his love for us. No human being can be as perfect in love for another as Jesus is in his love for us, but every human being can try. Husbands can try in the love they show their wives.

Julie*, may God grant that you find safety and security in John's* love for you. Let John's* love support you and set you free to be the person you want to be, as a wife, a mother, and someone God has given a very special life to live, and work to do in the world and in the home.

Amen.

Unromantic Love
Ephesians 5:21-33

Weddings are romantic occasions. There is the romance of candlelight, soft music, and lacy clothing. There are tender kisses, tears, smiles, hand-holding, and love songs. Weddings are pure, marvelous romance. That is what makes the Apostle Paul's words from Ephesians stand out like bib overalls on the best man.

On this romantic occasion, the words just read are anything but romantic. "Be subject" and "respect" sound like they belong in a social studies class. "Cleanse," "wash," and "nourish" could be from a recipe for cooking broccoli. The word Paul uses for "be subject" (Ephesians 5:21 NRSV) has also been translated "submit," which is about as unromantic as you can get and hardly belongs in company with the flowers and the songs that are giving this wedding its special beauty.

So far as we know, Paul didn't write these words for use in a marriage ceremony. Paul wrote them for use in a marriage relationship. He is speaking to the often unromantic work of two people building a life together, work that includes things like money, time, priorities, taking turns, raising children, deciding on which car to buy, which movie to see, which home to go to for Thanksgiving dinner, and how to disagree without being disagreeable.

As every married person here knows, the ongoing stability and goodness of the marriage relationship depends more on how these things are dealt with than on having candles on the dinner table and love songs on the radio.

When he uses the word love, the Apostle Paul does seem to introduce a bit of romance into what he has to say about marriage. When the word love is used at a wedding it creates a very romantic picture. Two people, our bride and groom*, have fallen in love. Wrapped in the love of family and friends here to celebrate their love with them, our bride and groom* promise each other the love that has brought them to this special moment will never end. This wedding, as every wedding should be, is all about romance and love.

The word love used in a wedding creates a very romantic picture. When the word love is used in a church, the picture it creates is anything but romantic. When we talk about love here in this church, we talk about a cross. We talk about Jesus being nailed to that cross and giving his life so that the world he is hurting with can be the world he shares heaven with. There is nothing romantic about the cross, nails, crown of thorns, agony of Jesus' pain, or the seeming hopelessness of Jesus' death. We don't see romance in that picture, but we do see love. We see the greatest love of all, God's love in Jesus, giving himself completely and sacrificing his life to bring goodness and blessing to our lives.

Marriage, your marriage John and Julie*, is about the romantic love that is visible in so many places on this good day. May both of you stay in this kind of love. May the kisses, soft words, gentle embraces, and simple joy of being together have a special place in all the years of your life together.

John and Julie*, your marriage is also about the very unromantic love that is shown to us on the cross of our Lord. May both of you bring that love to the life you build together. Bear each other's burdens. Share each other's pain. Support each other. Defend each other. Give of yourselves to bring goodness to each other.

Let the love for each other in your marriage come from Christ, his touch upon our troubled hearts is always more gentle than a lover's kiss. His commitment to building real goodness in our lives is as hard and forceful as the iron of the nails hammered through his hands. A good marriage ought to keep in it the gentle, romantic love we see in our wedding days. Even more, a good marriage must keep in it the strong, giving, unromantic love we see in Jesus giving himself for us on the cross.

John and Julie*, be gentle to each other in the love you show. Be strong for each other in the love you give.

Amen.

Out of Respect for Christ
Ephesians 5:21-33

"Be subject to one another out of reverence for Christ" (Ephesians 5:21). The first words of a piece of scripture often read at weddings. Although it is used a lot, I wonder if we really understand what it means. "Be subject" is sometimes translated as "submit." "Wives, submit to your husbands as to the Lord" (Ephesians 5:22 NIV). "Submit?" "Be subject?" Just what is it that the Apostle Paul is telling the Ephesians and us?

Let me give you some of the synonyms my Thesaurus[1] has for the words submission and subjection: "be a football," "be a mere machine," "be a puppet," "be driven into a corner," "be enslaved," "be led captive," "be trodden underfoot," "be in the clutches of," "be led by the nose," "be the plaything of," and, last but not least, the ever popular, "be henpecked." I may be wrong, but I don't think any of those expressions convey what the Apostle Paul is saying.

The Greek word Paul uses means "to arrange under." People in our society often feel they are in competition with one another. We buy books that tell us how to "win," how to be "number 1," or how to arrange things so that we, "come out on top" of the people around us.

Marriage is not immune from this kind of competition. Marriage sometimes becomes the primary battlefield of two people competing to arrange the relationship their own way so that they come out on top. We see this happening in marriages today. It seems as though Paul saw it happening in marriages in his day. That kind of competition is what Paul is speaking to in his letter to the Ephesians.

The picture is clear. When Christ looks at the lives of his people, he doesn't want to see us fighting and competing with each other, with all the pain, hurt, and frustration that brings. When Christ looks at how we live, he wants to see us joining together in companionship, loving each other, and working as partners for the common good.

Think of what Jesus does for you and me. Jesus loves us. Jesus gave his life for us. Jesus gives us a future beyond death, a future more wonderful than anything we can even imagine. It is at Jesus' request that our heavenly Father sends you and me the Holy Spirit, giving us the ability to live as children of God. We owe so much to Jesus. Out of respect for him and out of respect for our Lord we quit competing with each other and quit trying to come out on top in every situation. Out of respect for Christ, we do our best to live the way he wants to see his people live by arranging our living beneath the overarching togetherness we have in Jesus.

Marriage is not about competition. Neither is marriage about "submission." Marriage is about husbands and wives arranging their lives under the lordship of Christ. In that arrangement, out of respect for Jesus, husbands and wives have no interest in who is boss or who is the most important. All they want to do, all we married people want to do, is live together in love, the same kind of love Jesus has for us, putting our welfare ahead of his own and sacrificing himself for our salvation.

John and Julie*, in a few moments you will light the unity candle that symbolizes your "oneness," your togetherness, in marriage. Just as your individual candles serve the center candle of your togetherness, so let each of your lives "stand under" and serve the goodness and prosperity of your marriage. Out of respect for Christ, let him see you not as people fighting to win over each other. Let your Lord and Savior see you as people arranging their lives in such a way that you love, help, give, and sacrifice for each other.

Paul ends what he says about marriage with these two words: love and respect. John and Julie*, out of respect for Jesus, under his lordship, use those two words to arrange your life together in marriage. As you love and respect him, so love and respect each other, today, tomorrow, and always.

Amen.

---

1. *March's Thesaurus and Dictionary of the English Language*, Francis Andrew March and Francis A. March Jr. (Garden City, New York: Doubleday & Company, Inc., 1958).

Mutuality in Marriage
Ephesians 5:21-33

What the Apostle Paul is saying to husbands and wives in the fifth chapter of his letter to the Ephesians is often misunderstood. Paul isn't laying down rules for married life. Paul isn't saying, "John*, you are now Julie's* boss. Whatever you say goes." If you think that is what Paul is saying, then you misunderstand him. Julie* would never let you get away with that, anyway. Being Julie's* boss is not why you are marrying her. You are marrying Julie* because you love her and want to be her husband, companion, and friend.

"Julie*," Paul isn't saying, "here is the way things are going to be for you once you are married to John*. You are going to submit to him in everything. You are going to do whatever he tells you." Not only can't I picture you doing that, I know that John* doesn't want you as a submissive servant. John* wants you as a partner and as a wife who gives love, support, and help to him just as he gives love, support, and help to you.

In Paul's words to husbands and wives, Paul isn't laying down rules for married life. Paul is writing about mutuality in marriage. Paul is writing about how two people, how the two of you, John and Julie*, each contribute to making a good marriage. What Paul is saying is that it takes two. No husband, no matter how tough a boss he is, can make a good marriage by himself. No wife, no matter how submissive she is, can make a good marriage by herself. The heart and soul of marriage is interacting in love and companionship. For that to happen it takes two people — a husband and a wife — each making their special contribution to their life together.

In Paul's day, wives had a special contribution to make and husbands had a special contribution to make. What needed to be done by each of them to make a good marriage in the first century may not be true today. Just because Paul uses the words obedience and submissiveness to describe the contribution wives are to make in

148

marriage, does not mean we have to use those same words today. Today we don't include obedience and submissiveness when we talk about mutuality in marriage. Instead, we talk about love, mutual decision-making, mutual income-producing, and mutual home and family care-taking.

What is important for a good marriage is that each partner contributes to that marriage in their own special way. Each should honor and respect the special contributions made by their partner. In contributing to their marriage, each partner should do so in the name and example of Christ who out of love gave of himself without thought of receiving anything in return.

John and Julie*, in Jesus' name — helped and guided by God's word — each of you make your special contributions toward the goodness of your marriage. That is something you both need to do. That is something you both want to do. That is something Christ and his church is here to help you do. When you do that, your life together will be filled with love and companionship. That is what a good marriage is all about.

Amen.

Good Lessons for Life's Bad Days
Philippians 1:3-11; Matthew 5:38-48

Today is a good day. It is God's intent that every wedding day is a good day. God's word speaks to us on good days like this, the good days of our lives and the good days of our marriages. Unfortunately, we all know that every day in life is not a good day. As every married couple sadly and quickly learns, every day in life together is not a good day. God knows that, too, so God has things to say to us on the not good days of our lives, and the not good days of our marriages. That is exactly what the scripture lessons for this wedding do. On this good day, God speaks to us about life and marriage on the bad days.

It is no fun to be taken advantage of. It is no fun to be taken for granted. It is no fun to pay the price for someone else's bad moods. It is really no fun when the person doing those things is your spouse. As Jesus indicated to his disciples in our lesson from Matthew, you can either pay that person back with a little punishment of you own, "An eye for an eye, and a tooth for a tooth" (Matthew 5:38), or you can look into yourself for love, find it, reach into it, let it grow, and put it to work until it brings an end to the bad day and gives birth to another good day. Love has the power to do that. Often it is the only thing that can do that. When love isn't growing within marriages, bad days have a way of taking over.

We want our couple* to know that the best gift they can give to each other on their wedding day is their commitment to always keep love growing in their life together. In Christ, God has promised to always be there with his love, loving them and giving them love for each other to find, reach into, and let grow within them.

The Apostle Paul knew that about God. That's why Paul could write the way he did to the church members at Philippi. Paul was confident that all the love there for them in God would get them through the bad days they were having and bring them together into a new good day.

"I pray that your love will keep on growing more and more" (Philippians 1:9 GNB). That's what the Apostle Paul wrote in his letter to the church at Philippi. He wrote, "I pray that your love will keep on growing more and more."

Every day had not been a good day for the people in the church at Philippi. Every day had not been a happy day for them, as today is such a happy day for us. Church life is a lot like married life. Every day is not a good day. Every day is not a happy day. When Paul wrote to the church at Philippi, it was on one of those not so good and happy days. Some good people were having trouble getting along with each other. The whole church was feeling pretty down. It seemed like it wasn't much fun to be a church member.

Understanding that, Paul wrote, "I pray that your love will keep on growing more and more" (Philippians 1:9 GNB). Like Jesus, Paul knew that it is on the not so good and happy days that we need love the most. Maybe it isn't so front and center for us as it is on days like today, but God will make sure that love will be there for us to find. God will make sure that love will be there for us to reach into, and God will make sure love will be there to grow within us.

That's what Paul prayed for in the church at Philippi. That's what we pray for in the marriage of these two people*, that their love will keep on growing. When those bad, those not so good and happy days come along in their marriage, there will always be love for each of them to find, reach into, and put to work to bring those bad days to an end and let the new, good, and happy days arrive.

Let everyone here have the same confidence for our couple* Paul had for the church at Philippi that all the love is there for them in God will get them through any bad days that may come in their life together. Let us pray that finding love, reaching into that love, letting that love grow within them will bring them into new, good, really good and happy days of married and family life.

So we do for you two what Paul did for the people of the church at Philippi. We pray that your love will keep on growing. Those prayers are the best gift we can give you on your wedding day.

Amen.

Wedding Gifts and Their Care
Philippians 2:1-11

Just in case one of your guests has forgotten to buy you a wedding gift, I brought along a couple I am willing to sell cheap. See me after the service. The first gift I have is a coffee pot. The other gift is a plaque to put on the wall.

The coffee pot would make a nice gift. The one problem with a coffee pot is that it takes a lot of care. You have to put the filter in, put the coffee in, fill it with water, and turn it on. After you use it, you turn it off, dump the grounds, clean the filter, dump the leftover coffee, wash the basket, and wash the pot. A coffee pot is a nice gift, but if it is going to last and if it's going to keep brewing good coffee, it takes a lot of work. That's why the plaque may be just the kind of gift you want to give. Our couple* just has to nail this sweetheart to the wall and forget it.

God's word in Philippians describes marriage as a gift of God. God gives us this gift to meet our deep human need for companionship. God gives us the gift of marriage to make possible the building of families. Marriage is one of God's good gifts.

To some people marriage is like this plaque, beautiful, as today is beautiful, but after the gift is received you nail it to the wall and forget it. When the Bible talks about marriage, it describes it as a gift that is more like a coffee pot than a plaque. It is a great gift, but if it is going to last and if it is to continue to provide goodness, it is going to take some attention, care, prayer, and thoughtfulness.

In caring for a coffee pot, soap and water is what you use. In caring for a marriage, soap and water might have some usefulness, but they are not enough. In caring for a marriage we use the tools God provides. The same tools Jesus used so well: love, gentleness, kindness, humility, patience, compassion, and willingness to give of self for the sake of the other.

The two of you*, take good care of the coffee pots you receive as wedding gifts. Take even better care of what the wedding gift today is all about. God's gift to you of your marriage.

Amen.

Tuning Up a Marriage
Philippians 2:1-11

In our scripture lesson in Philippians, the Apostle Paul tells us that marriage is like the engine of a car.

Well, Paul doesn't use those exact words. He isn't talking about car engines. He isn't really talking about marriage either. What Paul is talking about are relationships. In so many words Paul is saying that relationships, especially marriage relationships, are a lot like the engine of a car. If they are going to be any good, they need to be kept in tune.

Tuning up a marriage is not quite the same as tuning up the engine of a car. For one thing, the tools are different. A torque wrench comes in handy when you are working on a car engine, but a torque wrench is not the tool of choice when you are tuning up a marriage. Then, too, when you tune up a car engine you often get grease on your hands. When you tune up your marriage, you often get tears in your eyes.

To be honest, the Apostle Paul didn't know a lot about car engines, but he did know a lot about people. Here in Philippians we have Paul's manual for tuning up a marriage.

The first thing husbands and wives have to do is to synchronize their minds. In a way that's like setting the timing on a car ignition. Anyway, two minds have to be synchronized to think as one. Two becoming one in marriage isn't just a nice idea. It is what makes a marriage run. Husbands and wives adjust themselves to see life through each other's eyes. A timing light won't help you do that, but Paul says that love will. Love is the tool. Husbands and wives use their love for each other to adjust their minds until they run as smoothly together as the cylinders of a car engine when it is perfectly in tune.

No good mechanic would tune up a car engine by pouring sand into the valves or salt water into the fuel pump. If a marriage is going to run the way it is supposed to, you don't put selfishness into it and you don't let ego turn partners into competitors. You sure don't gum up the works with "I'm always right, you're always wrong" conceit. What you use, Paul says, is humility. Both partners in the marriage, and to work it must to be both partners, become cheerleaders for each other. The cheer is never "hooray for me!" In a tuned up marriage, the cheer is always, "hooray for you!"

Now I'm not sure how good a mechanic the Apostle Paul might have been. I understand he was a whiz at making tents, but I don't suppose he ever worked on anything larger than chariot reigns or donkey harnesses. Paul did know what every good mechanic knows, a picture is worth a thousand words. You can write fifty pages on where to find the oil dipstick on any car, but just one picture of the engine block will serve the purpose. So, Paul says, if you want your marriage to work, you have to look like this. Then Paul shows us a picture of Jesus.

Take a good look at Jesus, Paul says. Your love should look like his love. Jesus devoted his life to serving our human needs. In the same way you each should be willing to serve the needs of the other. You should have the same contentment with being the person you are as Jesus had in being the person he was. Look at how Jesus' whole life was devoted to doing what God wants. Work on making your life look that way too. In love, Jesus sacrificed himself for all of us. When your love for each other requires it, be willing to sacrifice what you have in order to give your partner what they need.

For people who care about car engines, the most beautiful sound they can hear is the purring of an engine that is perfectly in tune. For people who care about relationships, the most beautiful relationships they can see are marriages where husbands and wives are living in that perfect "oneness" that has the look of Jesus about it.

Our prayer today for our bride and groom* is that they will use all the help God provides to make their marriage work as well, or better, than the engine of their car.

Amen.

The Mind of Christ
Philippians 2:5-8; Matthew 16:24-26

Marriage is about losing yourself in a relationship with another. "The two shall become one" (Matthew 19:5) is not some quaint old saying that has lost its meaning in today's world. Those words are the word of God concerning marriage. To God, marriage is about two people becoming one.

We receive these words from God as both law and gospel. As gospel, the words, "the two shall become one" reveal the wonderful gift God has given to us in marriage. "It is not good that the man should be alone" (Genesis 2:18). Those words in Genesis speak to our human need to have someone to share life with, to care, to listen, to love us and to be loved by us, and to share our hopes and dreams. It is one of life's greatest joys when we "become one" with that special person God has given us to be our companion in life. Its goodness is a gift. "Becoming one" in marriage is all about gospel.

"Becoming one" in marriage is also all about law. When God says, "The two shall become one," he is telling us what he expects married couples to do. They are to abandon their former individuality for the sake of their new unity. That is law and loss, two people losing who they were apart for the sake of who they are together. God knows what the world is like. Because God knows that the world we live in is filled with things that break people apart, God knows that for our own good in life, and especially in marriage, we need to be told we must do everything we can to stay together. Our hearts should tell us to do that. When they don't, we need God to tell us to do that in life and in marriage.

John and Julie*, in the scripture lessons you have included in your wedding we are being told to, "lose ourselves." Jesus means for us to lose ourselves in relationship to him. We are to give up doing what we want. Instead, we are to do what Jesus wants. What Jesus wants us to do in our marriages is to "become one."

In the scripture lesson from Philippians, we are encouraged to "let the same mind be in [us] that was in Christ Jesus" (Philippians 2:5). The Apostle Paul would have us do that everywhere in life. God would have us to that in our marriages. John*, love Julie* the same way Jesus loves her, forgive her, support her, encourage her, listen to her, celebrate her, and in every way she needs you, be there for her. That's how Jesus loves her.

John, that's the way Jesus loves you too. So, Julie*, "Let the same mind be in you that was in Christ Jesus," so that you love John* the same way Jesus loves him; with forgiveness, support, and encouragement. Listen to him and celebrate him. In any way John needs you, be there for him.

John and Julie*, never worry about what you might lose of yourselves by allowing the mind of Christ to direct your minds and thoughts about each other and about your life together in marriage. Whatever you might lose will be overwhelmed by the joy of what you will gain: Marriage as God intends marriage to be, full of goodness for you both.

Amen.

Rejoice
Philippians 4:4-9

It is a popular opinion that religion is a burden for people. The idea is that by belonging to an organized religion, like a church, you are loading yourself down with all sorts of responsibilities and obligations. To that picture of religion the response of many people is "Who needs it?" Some of you here at this wedding may feel that same way about religion.

I can't speak for every religion, but I can say this about the Christian church, to be a participant in it is not to be burdened. To be a part of what God is doing for the human family in Jesus Christ is to be set free. There is nothing in the world more wonderful than knowing you are included in all the goodness God is giving to the world through his Son, our Lord and Savior, Jesus Christ.

Martin Luther used to say that it is a good thing we humans never really believe all the good things God gives us in Jesus. If we did, he said, we would be so happy we would explode from joy.

Most of the time we Christians are our own worst enemies. We make our faith seem like a burden. We have to go to church. We have to follow all sorts of rules in the way we live our lives. We have to believe a certain way, talk a certain way, and think a certain way. When we read or teach the Bible, we seem to make it say that human happiness and human freedom ends when faith begins. When those around us see how burdened we act because of what we believe, they say "Who needs it?" What poor advertisers we are for our Lord and for what he has done for us.

To the Apostle Paul our Christian faith is all about freedom and happiness. In the scripture lesson read a few moments ago we heard Paul say, "Rejoice in the Lord always; again I will say, rejoice" (Philippians 4:4). Paul isn't saying that as a command, as though another thing Christians have to do is rejoice. When Paul says, "Rejoice," he is encouraging believers to release the joy that belongs to us because of Jesus.

That is what our Christian faith is to us, a gift of joy, a gift from God, who gives us joy when he gives us Jesus. It is the joy of being loved. It is the joy of being accepted as we are, not as something we have to be. It is the joy of knowing that all the things we do wrong are forgiven and forgotten because of all things Jesus did right. It is the joy of doing what is good and what is right not because we must, but because in Christ we can. It is the joy of knowing the whole human family is taken care of despite the fact that we are so poor at taking care of ourselves. It is the joy of having a wonderful future before us and Jesus is making sure we get there. Who needs that joy? You do, John and Julie*, you do and your marriage does.

Our Christian faith is a gift of joy from God to us in Jesus. It is the joy of having a companion as close as a whispered prayer. It is the joy of being invited into a community of people whose purpose is not to compete with each other but to encourage and support each other. Who needs that joy? You do, John and Julie*, you do and your marriage does.

Our Christian faith is a gift of joy from God to us in Jesus. It is the joy of being connected to all of life, to feel part of the earth, part of the sky, part of every living thing, and part of God. When we cry over all the pain in living now, over people suffering and people hurting, when we cry over so much that is not right in the way the world is, our crying is not the crying of hopelessness and despair. In our tears are the seeds of joy. We know God has not forgotten his broken world. We know with hope and confidence that God has made it his loving goal to turn every tear of sorrow, on every face on earth, into a tear of joy. Jesus gives us the joy of knowing he is coming to bring justice to the whole human race, living and dead. Who needs that joy? You do, John and Julie*, you do and your marriage does.

Our Christian faith is a gift of joy from God to us in Jesus. It is the joy of being free from every worry about ourselves, free to love our God and our neighbor with the enthusiasm that makes everything we do, no matter how hard, how thankless, how painful, the singing of a song of joy. Who needs that joy? You do, John and Julie*, you do and your marriage does.

Our Christian faith is a gift of joy from God to us in Jesus. That is the simple truth we have so much trouble making clear. Our Christian faith is a gift of joy. Every gathering for worship, every baptism and communion meal, every wedding, funeral, prayer, and expression of our faith is built of joy.

Who needs that? You do, John and Julie*, you do and your marriage does. Who else needs that? Every person here. We need that joy alive and at home within ourselves. We need that joy alive and at home in our marriages and in our families. The good news is that all that joy is ours as a gift of God, a gift he gives to us with the gift of his Son.

John and Julie*, in your life together find all the joy that God is giving you. Find it in worship. Find it in the reading of God's word. Find it in the prayers you pray and in the hope you share. "Rejoice," writes Paul. The joy God gives you is not something for you to hide. It is something for you to live each and every day in all the weeks, months, and years of your married life.

Amen.

Marriage Is Like a Gunny Sack
Philippians 4:4-9

John and Julie*, before I pronounce you husband and wife I want you to answer this question, "Is marriage like a cardboard box or is marriage like a gunny sack?" A right answer will get you a 10% discount on printed copies of this wedding sermon. A wrong answer will give me the choice of one of your wedding gifts. I warn you. I need a new toaster.

Actually, I think that marriage is much more like a gunny sack than it is like a cardboard box. You can't tell what is inside a cardboard box by looking at it. By looking, you usually can tell what is inside a gunny sack. If there is grain in a gunny sack, you can tell that by looking at it. Often you can even tell what kind of grain it is. Corn is rougher than something like oats. The outside of the bag would be bumpier. One thing about grain being in gunny sacks, some always seems to be sticking out of a seam or caught in the folds at the top. If there are nails in the sack you can tell by looking at the sharp points sticking out here and there. If it is rocks, fish, or a couple of chickens it shows on the outside of the sack.

If you put any of those things inside a cardboard box and closed the box, nothing would show. No one could tell by looking what was inside. You could wrap that box with the prettiest paper, make it the nicest looking thing around, and no one would know that inside there are two Northern Pike that are just at the point of going bad.

Marriage is like a gunny sack. Your marriage will show on the outside what the two of you are putting into it. If you put in anger, jealousy, violence, greed, abuse, or intimidation those things will show on the outside. Marriages in which those kinds of things are visible are not very attractive to look at. John and Julie*, we want your marriage to be as much a treat for our eyes ten years from now as it is a treat for our eyes today.

In the scripture lesson read a few moments ago, the Apostle Paul is telling you how to make that happen. Put inside your lives and marriage, "whatever is true, whatever is honorable, whatever is just, whatever is pure, whatever is pleasing, whatever is commendable, if there is anything worthy of excellence, and if there is anything worthy of praise" (Philippians 4:8). When those good things are put inside your marriage, your marriage will be a beautiful thing to see on the outside.

Today the two of you are the center of attention. It won't always be that way. Just because you are no longer the center of attention does not mean that these people will not be looking at you. They will be. Others will be too. Your marriage will never be like a cardboard box. What you put inside is going to show on the outside. May God help you fill your marriage with love and goodness. You need that on the inside. These people want to see that on the outside.

Amen.

Go Fish
Colossians 3:12-14

Being married is a lot like fishing. There are days when nothing is happening. There are days when the action never stops. There are days when you smile at each other and bait each other's hooks. There are days when you frown at each other while you try to get your lines untangled. There are days when you cheer together, because one of you landed a trophy. There are days when you laugh together, because what you thought was a ten-pound bass turned out to be someone's old waterlogged sweatshirt. Then there are days when all you can do is try to make the best of things in spite of the storm.

There are days on the lake when everything is as good as it can get: sunny sky, gentle breeze, the fish are biting, the deerflys are off somewhere biting someone else, and in the distance you can hear a radio playing love songs. There are days in marriage just like that. Love is everywhere you need it to be. God's love is shining down upon you. Your love for each other is drifting gently between you. Everything you do works out just fine. Life's problems seem a long way off. The sounds of the world around you make a kind of music, like a love song.

Marriages can have days like that. Those are the kind of days the Apostle Paul wants people to have in the lesson from his letter to the Colossians. Days of real caring for each other, caring that is felt in the deepest places of the heart. Days of kindness, when you each can't do enough to make your partner happy. Days of humility, when all you want is for your partner to feel proud and happy about themselves. Days when you sit quietly and let time go by just listening to your partner share their thoughts, feelings, hopes, and dreams. Days when neither partner gets annoyed by anything the other does. Days when husbands and wives look at each other knowing neither one is perfect, but also knowing it doesn't matter because, as it is with Jesus, forgiveness is a given. Days when the only thing that matters is love, all the love you have for yourselves from God, and all the love God gives you to use for one another. The Apostle Paul wants you to have days like that. God wants you to have days like that. Everyone here wants you to have days like that — good days when everything in your marriage is perfect.

Of course, as every person who's been fishing knows, not every day on the lake is a perfect day. Just the same, as every married person knows, not every day in married life is a perfect day. Every day, when you go fishing, you hope for the best, you plan for the best, and you work for the best. God wants us to do those same things in our marriages. Every day in our married lives God wants us to hope and plan for the best. Every day of our married lives God wants us to work for the best, putting to use his gift of love with all its compassion, kindness, humility, patience, and willingness to forgive.

Although fishing and getting married are alike in that both require a license, one way they are different is that in fishing there are limits, but not in marriage. God wants the two of you to know that there is no limit to the good days you can give to each other in your life together in marriage.

Amen.

Wedding Dress
Colossians 3:14

After reading the lesson our couple* has included in their wedding, and after carefully pondering over everything I have learned about relationships in all my years of ministry, I have reached the conclusion that the most important thing about a wedding ceremony and about marriage is the clothing.

I hope you don't think that sounds a little superficial. "What counts is not who you are. What counts is what the two of you wear." Experience tells me it's the truth. Without the right clothing a wedding can be a real disaster. That's why it is so important for couples to not only choose the appropriate clothing for their wedding day, but to show those clothes off so that rest of us can say to ourselves, "Those are nice clothes. I like those clothes. Those are the kinds of clothes I want to wear." A couple getting married should be real "trendsetters." Everyone should want to dress like them.

So the two of you* have a serious responsibility. The rest of us are paying careful attention to the clothes you are wearing today, but not only today. We will be paying just as careful attention to the clothes you will be wearing tomorrow, next week, next month, five years from now, twenty-five years from now, fifty years from now. You are going to have to pick out those clothes very carefully, just as carefully as you did when you selected the dress and tuxedo you are wearing now. You will need to order those clothes from a top designer. You will have to tailor them so they fit perfectly. You will want to get them in formal, casual, summer wear, winter wear, sportswear, work, and travel.

As a special favor to you, at no extra charge, I am going to give you the name of a man who can help you get those clothes wholesale, direct from the manufacturer. The man's first name is Paul. I don't know his last name. Some people call him Saul. He comes from the city of Tarsus, but you don't have to go there to find him.

You meet Paul in the Bible. You met him a few moments ago in the scripture lesson you included in your wedding. He wrote it. This is Paul's advice about what the two of you should wear as husband and wife. He says, "clothe yourselves with love" (Colossians 3:14).

Love is what the two of you have put on for your wedding day. Without that love, all the money spent on dresses and tuxedos has been wasted. It is love that gives your wedding its real beauty, its real style and grace.

It is your love the rest of us, your family and friends, came here to see. We need to see it in order to refresh our own love, so that husbands and wives here can look at each other and say, "Let's dress like this couple.* Let's put on our wedding clothes again." The love the two of you are wearing can help remind the rest us what our own wedding clothes really were. Our wedding clothes were not fabric, lace, and buttons. The real clothing we wore on our wedding day was love.

The thing about love is that love doesn't have to be returned like a tuxedo or hung in a closet like a wedding dress. The love you are wearing today, you can wear tomorrow, and through every day and week and year to come. Love is appropriate clothing for every occasion, at home, with family and friends, birthdays, anniversaries, Christmas, Easter, Memorial Day, even the Fourth of July. No matter where you are and what the occasion might be, you can't go wrong if you put on love.

One thing I should tell you about putting on love. You can't get it off the rack. The love you wear has to be tailor-made so that it fits you perfectly. You can't wear someone else's love. The way you care and help, the way you encourage and support, the way you understand and accept and forgive, all those things are uniquely your own. They come from love made-to-order.

The love you put on is received from God. God is its manufacturer. "If it doesn't come from God, it isn't love." That's what it says in the ads. God has even provided a catalog for you to look at. That catalog is the Bible. You find it in the four gospels: Matthew, Mark, Luke, John. In God's catalog you see Jesus modeling God's love. You see him modeling that love in all sorts of situations, happy ones and sad ones, in the city and in the country, privately with just a single person, publicly in crowds, and at a wedding. Another time he modeled God's love on a cross. If you want to know what you look like when you are wearing love, just look at Jesus.

The best thing about clothing yourselves in love is that the love you put on is free. It is a wedding gift for you from God. God's Holy Spirit has taken your measurements. The love each of you wears has been tailor-made and fits you to perfection. It is your wardrobe for a lifetime.

I pass on to you, and all your guests, this truth I have learned from experience. It is clothing that makes the wedding, and it is clothing that makes the marriage, but only when the bride and groom pick out and put on love.

Amen.

People of God
Colossians 3:12-17; 1 Corinthians 13

John and Julie*, speaking through his obedient servant, the Apostle Paul, your God has something special to share with you on the occasion of the beginning of your marriage. A few moments ago several verses from Paul's letter to the Colossians were read. In those verses God's word is speaking to all of us, the whole church of Christ. Now listen to those same words as God is speaking through them to the two of you as you begin your life together as husband and wife.

God addresses you as his "chosen ones" (Colossians 3:12). You are God's people. God wants you to know that. You are not your gender, your education, your occupation, or anything else that makes you different from each other. Both of you are people of God. That gives you perfect equality in your relationship. You each have the highest status anyone, man or woman, can achieve — that of being God's own child. Each of you has been chosen personally by God. Each of you is infinitely precious to God, making you that much more precious to each other, and equally precious to us, here with you on your wedding day.

What a great day this is, your coming together as two marvelous children of God. What a great day this is as the two of you celebrate the God-given wonder of each other. What a great day this is in your lives of mutual discovery, continuing to find all those special things in the way God has made each of you. Discovering them and promising before God to place everything special about yourselves forever at the service of your life together.

Having reminded you of your identity, and in so addressing you in the most noble manner as his special people, God describes your vocation — the life he has for the two of you. Noticeably absent from his description of your living are the things being sought by so many people in today's world. God says nothing about possessions, wealth, success, or status. God doesn't mention achievements or awards. God doesn't even talk about personal fulfillment or freedom for self-expression.

Actually God has already given you the highest level of personal fulfillment by merging your lives with the life of Christ. In Christ you each have the very best of what it means to be a human being. As for self-expression, there is nothing more meaningful than expressing the Christ who is within you, and who creates your authentic self, the person you really are, as God's own child. Neither of you has anything to prove to God, each other, or the world. Nothing you can ever do will add to or take away from what you already are in Christ. What you can do, what your vocation is, is to share with each other and with the world around you all the things that God has given you that make you who you are and give you the best of what you have.

Your vocation is to share forgiveness with each other and with the world around you. "Forgive us our debts, as we also have forgiven our debtors" (Matthew 6:12) is both a prayer and a way of life for you as God's people. Without the daily bread of forgiveness from God and from each other, we would all starve to death from loneliness. John and Julie*, God is giving you forgiveness as part of your daily bread. Pass it around at home to each other and away from home to all others. That is what God's chosen people do.

What God's chosen people do is to treat each other with compassion and kindness, humility and gentleness, and patience and acceptance. These are the things your lives are about. These are the things you are to give to each other and to share with each other. As God's special people they are the essence of who each of you are and what your marriage is about: compassion and kindness, humility and gentleness, patience and acceptance.

Don't forget love. That's what God is telling you as your marriage is beginning. "Above all, clothe yourselves with love" (Colossians 3:14). Love is just a word until it is given and shared, as Jesus gave and shared it, by caring more for another than for self. John and Julie*, when the wedding suits are returned to the store and the wedding dress is hung in the closet, clothe yourselves and your marriage with love. That is what God's special people do.

Peace is what God's special people have. Your Lord Jesus is giving you his peace to quiet your restless spirits and to calm whatever storms in life that might come. John and Julie*, in Christ God has given your hearts a place to rest. In your marriage be resting places for each other's hearts.

Be thankful because God has given you so much. God has given you his Son as your Savior. God has given you each other as lifelong companions. The hymn of thanks and praise to God should be the public song of every Christian marriage. It is a song for your lives to sing each and every day in all the years to come.

John and Julie*, you are God's people. God has chosen you and in Christ God has wrapped you and your marriage in his love. Live richly in that love. Give and share those essential things that belong to the people of God like compassion, kindness, humility, gentleness, patience, and forgiveness. In your life together let each of your hearts give and receive love, let each of your spirits give and receive peace, and as the gift of your life together, let God receive thankfulness. You are God's people and that is how God's people live. That is how God wants the two of you to live in marriage.

Amen.

Listening to God
Colossians 3:12-14

John and Julie*, a long time ago in a place much more rustic but more beautiful than this, two persons became husband and wife. In God's garden, the couple we know as Adam and Eve was united in a lifetime of companionship. It was the Bible's first marriage.

Despite not having things like microwave ovens, permanent-press clothes, or any clothes at all, Adam and Eve had things a lot easier than we do. Adam and Eve had only God to tell them how to live together in marriage. In today's world there are more people than we can count offering marital advice. Somewhere along the line each married couple has to make a decision about whose advice they are going to follow as they give shape to their marriage.

There are people telling us that in marriage, as in every relationship, we have to fight for our own rights and maintain our own individuality. We must not allow ourselves, or our behavior, to be shaped in any way by someone else. John and Julie*, the decision is yours about your willingness to listen to these people and let what they say shape your marriage.

There are people telling us that we must always follow the urging of our hearts. Marriage, they say, is only worthwhile as long as your heart is on fire with love. Should that warmth begin to cool, should that passionate heart glue begin to weaken, it is best to dissolve the union and follow your heart in a new direction. John and Julie*, there are people telling you that the voice in your heart is the only voice that matters. The decision is yours about your willingness to listen to those people.

There are people around who tell us that the only thing worth living for is our personal fulfillment, measured by successful performance in the economic world. To prove we have the stuff of winners in our blood we must be willing to sacrifice every relationship including those in marriage and family. John and Julie*, there are people telling you that in climbing the ladder of success you must consider your relationship to each other as disposable. Once again, the decision is yours about your willingness to listen to those people and let what they say shape your marriage.

Adam and Eve only had to listen to God. How much easier that must have been. In today's world, crowded as it is with people giving their advice about life and marriage, every married couple has to make choices about who they are going to listen to. John and Julie*, when you began to make plans for your wedding, you made a choice about where that wedding would take place. You chose to be married in this church. One of the things we do in this church is listen to the word of God. The word we have listened to today is from the third chapter of the Apostle Paul's letter to the Colossians:

> As God's chosen ones, holy and beloved, clothe yourselves with compassion, kindness, humility, meekness, and patience. Bear with one another and, if anyone has a complaint against another, forgive each other; just as the Lord has forgiven you, so you must forgive. Above all, clothe yourselves with love, which binds everything together in perfect harmony.
>
> (Colossians 3:12-14)

Those words are the word of God. As God spoke to Adam and Eve in the garden, so has God spoken to us today. The two of you have made the choice to listen.

May you make that same choice as you shape your lives together as husband and wife. Listen to God as God speaks to you about love, kindness, and trust. Listen to God as God speaks to you through his Son, Jesus Christ. Listen to God as God speaks to you through his Bible and through his church.

As you chose to listen to God today, may you listen to God every day. May you listen and may you use what you hear from God in the building of your life together. There are all sorts of voices speaking to us in today's world, but for the well-being of our lives, and the well-being of our marriages, the voice we need most to listen to is the voice of God.

Amen.

Children of God
(Two Successful People)
Colossians 3:12-17

Who are you? John and Julie*, we know your names, but beyond those identifying labels, who are you? In a world crowded with people, who are you?

Let's see if we can tell who you are by your appearance. You are clean people. That's nice. You are neat and well-groomed. Perhaps the two of you are slightly overdressed, but that is understandable on your wedding day. We can see those things, but they don't really tell us who you are.

Maybe we can tell who you are by your manners. Standing here so cool and calm in front of all these people tells us that you have a lot of self-confidence. The way you are conducting yourselves displays a lot of maturity and sophistication. Whoever you are, there is much about you to admire.

Your achievements are good evidence that both of you are capable people, outstandingly so. Your academic records reveal that you are well-educated. Your employment records tell us that both of you are successful in the business world. By projecting your future we can be reasonably sure you will be prosperous people, with a nice home and nice things.

It seems as though we do know a lot about you, but do we *really* know who you are? Maybe God's word can tell us that. Maybe God's word does tell us that in the lesson read a few moments ago. In writing to the baptized community in Colossae the Apostle Paul refers to them as "God's chosen ones" (Colossians 3:12). If Paul were writing to you, he would address you the same way, because that is who you are. You are "God's chosen ones." In Christ, the two of you are God's children.

God's word tells us that whatever else there is to know about you we know this, and you know this about yourselves, you are God's chosen ones. You are children of God. You are embraced by the strong love of your Creator. You are warmed by the peace-giving love of your Savior. You are renewed by the love-giving presence of God's Holy Spirit. That is who you are. That is what your lives and your lives together in marriage are all about. After your wedding you will change your clothes, but in all the changes the future will bring, this one thing will always be the same. Forever and beyond, you will be God's chosen ones. You will be children of God.

In telling you who you are on your wedding day, God's word tells you how you are to live your married life. "As God's chosen ones holy and beloved, clothe yourselves with compassion, kindness, humility, meekness, and patience. Bear with one another and, if [either of you] has a complaint against [the other], forgive each other; just as the Lord has forgiven you, so you must forgive. Above all, clothe yourselves with love" (Colossians 3:12-14).

John and Julie*, you know who you are in the business world. You know what you need to do to be successful there. In your lives, and in your life together in marriage, you are children of God and God wants you to know what you need to do to have a successful marriage. In addition those qualities of love, kindness, and the rest, let the "peace of Christ rule in your hearts" (Colossians 3:15), and let the peace of Christ rule in your home. Be grateful to God and grateful to each other. Make God's word a regular part of your living and worship a regular part of your week.

John and Julie*, God wants you both to know who you are — his chosen ones — his children. God does not want that to be a burden for you, a duty for your marriage. God wants that to be a joy for you, a joy for your marriage, and a joy for your family. You are children of God and that gives you wonderful things to know, wonderful things to sing about, and wonderful things to share.

John and Julie*, you are God's children. That is who you are. That is good reason for you to "do everything in the name of the Lord Jesus" (Colossians 3:17). That is what God's children do in their lives and in their marriages.

Amen.

So Much to See
(Outdoor Wedding)
2 Thessalonians 3:5

What a beautiful view we have here today. There is so much to see. The wonderful mix of colors as the season changes. Birds in flight across a clear blue sky. A dancing sparkle off the breeze-swept water. Here and there families are enjoying the beauty of the day.

So much to see; yet, we have no problem knowing where to look. Our eyes are on these two people*. Our eyes are on them — the two of them together. So much to see, but we cannot take our eyes off the couple, at least not for long. They are the center of our attention.

There is so much for us to see in God's word — the Bible. There are wonderful stories of creation, the flood, and the Exodus from Egypt. Stories about David and Goliath; Daniel in the lion's den; Shadrach, Meshach, and Abednego in the fiery furnace.

There is so much for us to see in the Bible. There are so many people; Adam and Eve, Abraham and Sarah, Moses, Joshua, David, Solomon, Mary the mother of our Lord, and Mary Magdalene, Peter, and Paul.

There is so much for us to see in the Bible. There are so many beautiful verses, "This is the day that the Lord has made; let us rejoice and be glad in it" (Psalm 118:24). "The Lord is my shepherd, I shall not want" (Psalm 23:1). "All things work together for good for those who love God" (Romans 8:28). "Come to me, all you that are weary and are carrying heavy burdens, and I will give you rest" (Matthew 11:28). "I can do all things through [Christ] who strengthens me" (Philippians 4:13).

There is so much for us to see in the Bible, in the 66 books that make up the written word of God. Yet we have no problem knowing where to look, at least if the hope of the Apostle Paul is realized in our lives, "May the Lord direct your hearts to the love of God" (1

Thessalonians 3:5). Paul wants us to look at love, God's love, the story of God's love, the story told to us in his Son, Jesus our Lord, who loved us so much that he gave his life for us.

In the Bible we look at Jesus, God's saving love, born in Bethlehem, growing to the man who healed, who welcomed, who had a special place in his heart for the lonely and the forgotten. Even though there is so much to see in the Bible, it is love that captures our attention, "For God so loved the world" (John 3:16) and "just as I have loved you, you should also love one another" (John 13:34).

There is so much to see in marriage. Yet the two of you* should have no trouble knowing where to look. Look at love. Look at your love, God's love, love to receive, love to give, love to fill a home, love to share with friends and neighbors.

All these people who have their eyes on the two of you today will continue to look at you in your life together. They will be looking at you through the changing seasons of your marriage. Whenever they look, let them see love.

Amen.

Sculpting a Marriage
1 Timothy 6:17-19

A long time ago a gray headed old man gave some advice about life to his young friend. I may not be as old as the Apostle Paul, nor as wise, but I share his gray hair and I pass along his advice to you young friends. Do not set your hope "on the uncertainty of riches, but rather on God who richly provides us with everything for our enjoyment" (1 Timothy 6:17).

John and Julie*, your married life will soon begin to take its shape and form. As an artist molds the clay to form a figure, so will the two of you mold the figure of your marriage. You will do that by how you live, the decisions you make, the love (or lack of it), you share with each other and with those around you in the world. In the next few months and years this shape you give to your marriage will harden. Its form will become permanent. It happens that way to people.

So the critical time is now; the coming days and weeks, the next few months, the next few years. What shape are you going to give to your life together? Like so many, will you be going after the riches of the world? Will the shape of your married life be dominated by two pairs of enormous hands reaching out to encompass the big car, big home, big money, and shining riches of this richest of countries? Will the shape of your married life be dominated by two huge gaping mouths, open to devour, selfishly and greedily, everything that comes in reach?

Those shapes and forms of married life, ugly as they are, are not uncommon in our society. The hands are the hands of Adam and Eve, reaching for the divine wealth of the forbidden fruit. The mouths are the mouths of Adam and Eve, open to devour the garden itself.

Be careful so that you don't give these shapes to your life together. Be careful so that you don't let those distorted human forms of greed and selfishness harden around you and become the permanent image of who you have chosen to be as husband and wife.

There is another shape for the two of you to give to your married life. It is the form of two people facing each other in love. The arms of these two people are extended toward each other. Each person holds one hand palm upward, open to receive with gratitude the gifts God so generous provides for them. Each person's other hand is open palm outward, bent to pour from their abundance a share for those around them in the world.

That is the shape you can give to your life together. It is formed by hope set upon God, upon God's love, and upon God's generosity in the basics of life: air, water, sunlight, work to be done, love to be shared, people to be known, a word of good news in Jesus Christ to be celebrated. There is so much goodness God will be giving you. As husband and wife, let your hands be always open in gratitude to receive it.

Shape your life together around God's goodness for the whole of his creation. Work together in the world as the people God created you to be, people who tend his garden and not plunder or devour it. As husband and wife, do not shake your fists at the world; open your hands and your hearts.

John and Julie*, like an artist beginning to give shape and form to a piece of clay, you are now beginning to sculpt your married life. The coming days and weeks and the next few months and years will be critical in giving your life together its shape and form. Build your marriage in the image of children of God. Face each other in love and open your hands in gratitude as you receive God's gifts. Reach out your hands in charity, as you share God's generosity with your brothers and sisters in the world.

You are the artists. Your marriage is the clay. Be careful as you give it shape and form. Be careful and be faithful.

Amen.

God's Good Gifts
James 1:17-18

What do a polluted stream, a soaring divorce rate, and a broken family have in common? They are all results of what people do to the good gifts of God. As James writes in our scripture lesson, God is a giver of good gifts, "Every good gift, and every perfect present comes from heaven" (James 1:17 TEV).

The gifts God gives are good as only God can make them. There is the clear water of a stream sparkling in the sunlight. A man, tired from a long day working in his field, dips his cup into that stream and lifts the cup to his lips. Clear, fresh water, what a gift, what a marvelous gift from God to a thirsty world.

A husband and wife are offering each other companionship. Neither one being slave nor master, each being a friend and lover. Two people making and working faithfully to keep promises of building their lives together for the support and well-being of one another. Marriage, as God established marriage to be, what a gift, what a marvelous gift of companionship God has given to a lonely, often selfish, world.

The deep interpersonal sharing of a family, the growing together, the meeting of each other's needs, the self-sacrifice that gain rewards that money could never buy. Families living in the safety, security, and stability in which physical and emotional needs of members are met by those who care. The family, as God created families to be, what a gift, what a marvelous gift of God to an impersonal, often uncaring, world.

"Every good gift and every perfect present comes from heaven" (James 1:17 NIV). God is a gift-giver. The gifts he gives us are good as only God can make them good. Unfortunately the goodness of those gifts can sometimes be taken from them. The stream is polluted, its water undrinkable. The marriage is ended. The pleasure it once provided turned to pain. The family goes to pieces, creating emotional damage instead of healing it. Taking the goodness out of the gifts God gives is the devil's work, but we can't make Satan take all the blame. It is people work too.

People, you and I, can pollute the stream. People can turn marriage companionship into marital competition. People can turn family stability and security into a struggle for the survival of the fittest. People can do some really awful things to the gifts God gives us.

Maybe we forget where those gifts come from. Maybe we separate the gifts from the God who gave them. Once we take God's gifts into our own hands, there is no one to prevent us from doing what we want to them. What we want is not always what God wants.

Maybe we forget that the gifts are meant to be good. If we don't see the goodness in them, we have no reason to treasure or protect them and use the best of our abilities to tend and nurture them. Simple neglect can be simply awful in the damage it can do.

John and Julie*, this marriage is a gift of God. There is a lifetime of goodness in it for you. There is so much goodness God is giving you. There is so much goodness that you, in your marriage, have to give to family, friends, community, and God's creation.

Always remember that your marriage is God's gift to you. Live out your marriage as God wants you to. Love each other the way God loves you. Remember Jesus and how God gave his Son to you, not counting his cost but meeting your need. In your marriage God wants you each to give of yourselves to meet each other's needs. In the book of Genesis, God had work for Adam to do. Adam's work was to tend the Garden. Adam's work is your work too. The Garden is your marriage. Your work is to tend it so that the goodness of your marriage will continue to grow and blossom.

John and Julie*, always remember that your marriage is a good gift. Your marriage is a precious treasure, worth all the time and attention necessary to protect and preserve it. Do that and your marriage will glow brighter and brighter, lighting your lives and shining its goodness on the lives of those who surround you in the world.

God gives good gifts. Your marriage is one of those gifts. Today is a day for you to enjoy its goodness. May you tend your marriage so that its goodness can be enjoyed in all the days, weeks, months, and years to come.

Amen.

Relationships: A Scientific Study
James 3:2-12; Matthew 6:25-34; Genesis 2:18-24; 1 Corinthians 12:31—13:13

In today's world where so few of life's mysteries remain unexamined, it should come as no surprise that science has found a way to calculate precisely, by empirical observation, the state of the relationship between a man and a woman.

It began in the 1950s with the "Bench Front Seat" theory. This theory held that a studied glance at a couple in the front seat of an automobile could determine the state of their relationship. This could be done as follows:

Boy with left elbow out the left window. Girl precisely between the transmission hump and the passenger door, with hands on lap. (First Date)

Boy with right elbow on seat back. Girl having bisected the previous distance between transmission hump and self. (Third Date)

Boy with right arm fully stretched on seat back. Girl directly above transmission hump. (Going Steady)

Boy and girl both occupying driver's side of the seat. Girl's head nearly invisible, having melted into the boy's shoulder. (Engaged)

Same as above, with tin cans tied to the rear of the car. (Just Married)

Boy and girl each in mid-seat position, separated by a child in a car seat, which has its own plastic steering wheel. (Second Anniversary)

Man with left elbow out left window. Woman with right elbow out right window. Several feet of the front seat now separating the two of them. (Typical Married Couple)

Individual front seats, along with seat belt and child restraint laws, have rendered the front seat theory obsolete. Technology, however, will find its way. The present method of dating relationships has shifted from what is visible to what is audible. Without an extensive elaboration on phonetics, inflection, and harmonic distortion, I can tell you that the theory is based on the number of times the word love is exchanged and the number of times the unmistakable sound of kisses can be heard. Both sounds are introduced hesitantly at first, reach a crescendo during the going-steady, engagement, and just-married period, and recede into near silence as the marriage progresses.

It is at this point, John and Julie*, that we begin to talk about your relationship, especially with respect to the lesson from James that was read a few moments ago. Here in his letter, James is concerned with how people talk to each other. A critical element in your marriage relationship will be how you, as a couple, talk, or fail to talk, to each other. As James warns, and as experience demonstrates, unless you pay attention to the language in your marriage that language will go off in its own and sometimes unpleasant directions.

The direction you want the language of your marriage to take is shown in Genesis 2. It is the language of companionship. It is a way of talking to each other that drives away loneliness. It is language used to bring your lives closer together. Never forget that words in marriage can be used to add to loneliness. Words can become bricks by which walls will be built between you. The language of companionship is God's garden gift to the two of you. Tend and nourish this precious gift through the full season of your life together.

In our Matthew lesson, Jesus tells us that our thoughts and our language are not to be focused on all the causes for worry and anxiety in our lives. Instead we should think about and talk about the goodness of our daily living within our heavenly Father's promised care. It is possible for language in marriage to sound like the conversation in the executive boardroom of a corporation about to declare bankruptcy. John and Julie*, that is not the sound you want to hear in your life together, not when there is so much you have to talk about that has to do with faith, hope, trust in God, and gratitude for goodness found in simple things. It is in those things that the language of your marriage should be anchored.

Finally in his letter to the Corinthians, the Apostle Paul puts language and behavior together in one word. That word is love. Somehow, in some way, the language of love must be kept alive in marriage. If it is not there in the way husbands and wives talk to each other, it will not be there in the way husbands and wives treat each other.

John and Julie*, pay good attention to the biblical language of love as that love flows freely from God to you. Weekly worship and home devotions will help to make that happen. The rest will come about with care, prayer, and commitment to maintain the love language you want your marriage to have. Language without behavior is not enough, of course. In your marriage each will depend upon the other. In your lifelong conversation with each other as husband and wife, the love in the things you do will flow and lead back to the love in the words you speak.

John and Julie*, in your marriage do your best to keep the experts guessing. When curious scientists study your conversation during the next month, the next year, the next ten, or twenty years, talk to each other in such a way that the sounds they record will cause their computers to print out that the two of you are newlyweds.

Amen.

Instructions
1 Peter 3:1-11; 1 Corinthians 13:1-8, 13

John and Julie*, your marriage is like a toaster. When a toaster works the way it is supposed to work, it brings happiness to your breakfast. When your marriage works the way God created marriage to work, it brings happiness to your life.

When marriage works the way God created marriage to work, it brings a companionship that eases the loneliness that exists at the deepest level of human living. When marriage works, it brings people a sense of fulfillment, a place for them to give the very best that is within them and a place to receive from another the best they have to give. When marriage works, it delivers an endless supply of goodness to the daily living of all those involved: husband, wife, children, family, and friends.

When marriage works the way God created marriage to work, it brings happiness. John and Julie*, when your marriage works, it will bring happiness to you. The question for every married person is, "How can marriage work the way God created it to work?"

In the two scripture lessons read a few moments ago, the Apostles Peter and Paul offer instructions for marriage. Husbands, Peter says, have a certain role to play in making marriage work. The same is true for wives. Wives, says Peter, also have a certain role to play in making marriage work.

It would be easy if today's husbands and wives could make their marriages work by following Peter's specific instructions. The trouble is that Peter's instructions relate to the culture of 2,000 years ago, and how husbands and wives could make their marriages work in that time and place. We can listen to what Peter says and learn from him, but as I said before, marriage is like a toaster.

If you want your toaster to make the best toast possible, you begin by reading the instructions. After you read the instructions, you work with the controls, make all the necessary adjustments so that the bread is toasted just the way you like it. Marriage is like a toaster. First you read the instructions, like those Peter is giving in his letter, then you work on your relationship making the necessary adjustments to provide husbands and wives with goodness and happiness.

Instructions are important in making toast and in being married. Instructions are important but in making toast the way you like it, and in making marriage work the way God created marriage to work, you have to do more than read the instructions. To make marriage work you have to pay attention to the relationship, care about how it is going, and take responsive action to make the adjustments that keep the marriage going well.

The tools you use to make adjustments on your toaster are your fingers. The tool you use to make adjustments on your marriage is your love. To paraphrase the Apostle Paul in our scripture lesson from 1 Corinthians, "If I have the best instructions for marriage, but am without love, the instructions are a waste of time." Love provides the patience, kindness, humility, forgiveness, courage, faith, and commitment, married couples use as they make those adjustments to keep the marriage working well.

One of the things I have learned from our toaster is that the adjustments we needed to make were not only when we began to use it. If we want our toaster to continue to make toast just the way we like it, we continue to make adjustments. As life together goes on in marriage, couples need to continue to use God's gift of love to make adjustments in their relationship. That is the way their marriage will continue to produce happiness.

John and Julie*, one of the guests at your wedding will probably give you a toaster. Think of the happiness you both are going to have when you open the box, read the instructions, plug in your toaster, adjust the controls, and make toast just the way you like it. Another guest at your wedding, God's Holy Spirit, is giving you the gift of love. Think of how happy you are both going to be when you use that love in making those adjustments in your relationship, which will keep your marriage producing just the kind of goodness you like for the rest of your lives.

Amen.

Sacrificial Love
1 John 4:7-19

In his letter to the church, John tells us that we are to love one another as God loves us. That kind of love involves sacrifice. That's the way it is with God's love. God the Father loved us so much he gave, sacrificed, his only Son.

Now in some marriages one partner sacrifices their own happiness because they think that will make the other person happy. That's not a good idea. It is certainly not the kind of sacrifice anyone here wants either of you to make. I don't believe it is the kind of sacrifice God wants either of you to make, giving up your own happiness to make your partner happy. When, out of his love for us, God gave his only Son, God did not sacrifice his happiness. God found his happiness in the new relationship he created with us because of the sacrifice he made. God's love made its sacrifice for the sake of our life together with him. He acted to bring happiness to us. That brings happiness to him.

Today the two of you, our bride and groom*, are committing yourselves to a lifetime of love. That means a lifetime of sacrifice, sacrifice in the service of love. For the rest of your lives each of you will find your happiness in the happiness you bring to each other. The love you are committing yourselves to is a love that says, "I must do whatever I can, make any sacrifice necessary, so that our marriage is as good as it can be." There is happiness for you both in the goodness each of you can bring to your life together.

In his letter to the church at Corinth, the Apostle Paul describes how sacrificial love is lived out in life together. He describes it as being patient and kind, not envious, boastful, arrogant, or rude. Love, for Paul, does not insist on its own way, is not irritable or resentful, does not rejoice in wrongdoing, but rejoices in the truth. Love, as God gives it to be used by us, "bears all things, believes all things, hopes all things, endures all things" (1 Corinthians 13:7). That kind of love, in life and in marriage, requires sacrifice. It is a way for us to love one another the way God loves us. It is a way to bring happiness and goodness to our life together.

God wants both of you to have that happiness and that goodness in your marriage. All of us here today want both of you to have that happiness and goodness in your marriage. I have no doubt that both of you want that happiness and goodness in your marriage. It is love that makes that happen, love that involves sacrifice, sacrifice in the service of love, loving one another as God, in Christ, loves you.

The goodness and happiness that is there for each of you in your life together is worth every sacrifice you make. That isn't just something I am saying in my marriage sermon. That is something you will be discovering in your married life. The goodness and happiness that you share in your marriage is worth every sacrifice you make.

The two of you, our bride and groom*, love one another as God loves you.

Amen.

Important Things
1 John 4:7-21

Marriage is an important thing. We make jokes about it. We surround it with all sorts of silliness. With all the running around, our wedding days have something of a circus about them. All that being true, it does not change the fact that marriage is an important thing. We all know that. Beneath the jokes and silliness, we all feel that importance. As we go about our living in this world, getting married, being married, and staying married are among the most important things we do. What are some of the others?

What is a "most important thing" a person can do? Someone might say, "The most important thing you can do is enjoy yourself." That's one answer, and it's a good answer. God has created each of us in such a way that there are things about ourselves we can enjoy. By enjoying ourselves we honor our Creator. God has created the world in such a way that there is a lot in the world, and a lot in other people, to be enjoyed. When we enjoy what God has made, without misusing it, we honor our Creator.

"Enjoying yourself" as and in God's creation is one of the important things a person can do, but it is not *the* most important thing. Most of us understand that there is more to living than enjoying ourselves, but if that is not *the* most important thing a person can do, what is?

"Being happy" might be an answer. That, too, is a good answer. An unhappy person is a great weight on life, pulling down everything around them. It is good to be happy with yourself. It is good to find happiness in your marriage. It is good to find happiness with your friends. It is good to find happiness in your job. It is good to find happiness in the things you do for fun. It is good to find happiness in the help and support you are able to bring to others. It is especially good to find happiness in the bond of love God has made with you in his Son, our Lord and Savior, Jesus Christ. Finding happiness in those things is not only good for you, it makes the people who share your space feel good too. Being happy is a very important thing; we all know that, just as we know or should know that it isn't *the* most important thing.

Maybe "taking charge" is the most important thing a person can do. The world needs people who don't just "go with the flow." The world needs people who make things happen and accept responsibility for what they do. When taking charge isn't just a way of pushing other people around, but a way of putting your best to work, it is a very important thing for everyone, for husbands and wives, parents and children, everyone. Still, it isn't *the* most important thing a person can do. None of us is capable enough so that when we take charge we can handle everything.

The Bible has two answers to the question of the most important thing a person can do. The first answer is "accept the love God has shown for you in Jesus." That is letting God do what God does best, rescue the world he created, loves, and gave his Son to save. The most important thing any of us can do is to do nothing, simply get out of the way and allow God to do it all, as his love accomplishes our salvation and the salvation of the world. "Accept God's love for you," is the Bible's first answer to the question of the most important thing a person can do. The second answer is, "make love work for others."

The voices of the Apostles John and Paul echo the voice of Jesus himself, giving God's word the clear instruction to us all that the most important thing any of us can do is respond to God's love for us by putting love to work for others. The most important thing God is doing is everything his love does for us in Jesus. The most important thing we can do is put love to work everywhere in our lives: love at work in our marriages, love at work in our families, love at work for our friends, love at work for our companions on the job, love at work for all the people sharing space with us, in our neighborhood, and on God's earth.

For the two of you,* this day of your wedding is a most important day. The life you will be sharing together in marriage and family is a most important thing. I join your family and friends in hoping that you will always enjoy yourselves and enjoy each other. We hope you will always be happy and that your happiness with each other will grow day by day. We encourage you to take charge and make good things happen for each other, for us, and for those who will be part of your lives in the years to come. Those are some of the most important things we want for you both.

But *the* most important thing we want for you is that you will always know how much God loves you, you will always know what his love means for you, and you will never stop putting love to work everywhere in your lives, especially in your marriage.

Amen.

Knowing God
1 John 4:7-12

Marriage, love, and life as God's people are the themes that intertwine in this place today. They encircle John and Julie* as they stand arm in arm, to be united together as husband and wife. Marriage, love, and life as God's people is what they are talking about when they speak their vows to each other. That is what they are expressing today, as they place themselves, their love, and their marriage in the creative and supportive hands of God.

Marriage, love, and life as God's people. Those themes co-mingle among us all as each of us reflects upon the place of love in our lives, our commitments to one another as husbands and wives, family members, and neighbors and friends. How does our love and our loving commitments to others relate to our life as God's people?

Among the words in the scripture lesson is this statement: "Everyone who loves is born of God and knows God... for God is love" (1 John 4:7-8). That is an astonishing assertion. If you consider it, you will realize how much it goes against the grain of our natural assumptions. The normal procedures for knowing God are: reading the Bible, going to church, participating in programs of Christian education, and engaging in conversation with other believers. Those are the methods by which we all seek to know God.

In our scripture lesson, John is telling us that we don't know God that way. True, by doing those things we may learn to know information about God, but we do not know God. According to John, we know God only when we love others. So it is that the themes at this wedding service are welded inseparably together in Christian marriage — marriage and love and life as God's people.

Our life as God's people is measured not by the sincerity of our faith, the quality of our service to the church, the depth of our learning, or the respectability of our conduct. Our life as God's people is measured by only one thing: our love for the people with whom we share our lives in this world.

That love is never abstract or generalized. It is love practiced between husbands and wives in marriage. It is love practiced between parents and children. It is love practiced between members of Christ's church. It is love practiced between people who are bound by the strongest commitment of all, to love all those whom God loves. This means the love we are to put in practice extends to everyone and to every nation on this planet and beyond.

Those who put this love into practice know God. Those who do not put this love into practice do not know God, no matter the amount of information they may have learned about him.

So, John and Julie*, grow together in your knowledge of God, grow in the reality of the love you put into practice within your relationship to each other and grow in the reality of the love that extends from that relationship into the lives of the people around you in family, community, church, and all creation. Daily devotions together, weekly worship, study of God's word, and Christian teaching are additions to, not replacements of, love as your way of knowing God. Doing those good and important things will lead you into a deeper understanding of God's truth, God's will, God's justice, a deeper understanding of yourselves as children of God, and a deeper understanding of what it means for you to accept God's truth, follow his will, and work on God's behalf. It is always good to learn more about God, because when you learn more about God you learn more about his love. Learning more about God's love is the best way to learn more about yourselves.

Julie and John*, may your marriage be a lifetime learning experience for you both. May you continue to grow in your understanding of all the ways love is to be put into practice for each other. May you continue to grow in your understanding of all the ways the two of you can put your love into practice for others. As that happens in your marriage you will know God in that special way God is known by partners in a Christian marriage. May love, marriage, and life as God's people, the themes woven together on your wedding day, create the fabric of your life together as husband and wife.

Amen.

Love Each Other
1 John 4:7-21

John and Julie*, today the two of you are the center of attention. It isn't often in life that we are the center of attention for more than a handful of people. Today a tremendous amount of attention is being centered on you. All these people here have their attention focused on you. I have my attention focused on you. In the lesson from the Bible that has just been read, God's word is focused on you. God's Holy Spirit is focused on the two of you in a special way as you make your vows and receive God's blessing.

All this attention is bound together by a single desire. That desire can be summed up in three words, "love each other." All these people here want both of you do that. These people want you to love each other, not just today, but in all the days, weeks, months, and years to come. Everything I say and do in this wedding service and celebration has a single purpose: that for the rest of your lives the two of you will accept the love God has for you and that you will love each other.

In the scripture lesson from 1 John, God's word encourages, inspires, and commands you to "love one another" (1 John 4:7). God's Holy Spirit, who brings God's gift of love to all of us, is at work to build a loving presence within each of you — a loving presence that will reach out in daily expression of your love for each other.

Love each other. That is the common desire that surrounds the two of you today. Love each other. Love each other romantically. Touch and whisper, kiss and hug. That good, warm love belongs in your life together. Love each other carefully. Take loving care of each other. Love each other sacrificially. Let the measure of your love be in how much each of you gives from yourself for the sake of the other. Love each other prayerfully. Pray often and remember each other in your prayers. Love each other as true companions. Marriage was God's answer to human loneliness. Let your love for each other be the answer to any loneliness that either of you might feel.

John and Julie*, there is one special thing all these people here today hope you will do. There is one special thing I want you to do. There is one special thing God's word tells you to do. There is one special thing God's Holy Spirit is helping you to do. That one special thing is for you to love each other. Love each other for the rest of your lives.

Amen.

Beautiful Words
1 John 4:7-21

"Beloved, let us love one another" (1 John 4:7). Beautiful words from someone who must have been a beautiful person. His name was John. He wrote about love. John knew all about love. He learned it from the most famous lover in history, Jesus Christ.

"Let us love one another," John wrote. The words John wrote in Greek are even stronger than the English translation suggests. John was not offering people a suggestion. John was giving people a command. "Friends," he was saying, "we have to love each other."

Look at the world. Read the newspaper. Watch the evening news. Check out the list of divorces in the court records. See the battered women, the suicides, the crowds who abandon hope for the forgetfulness of drugs and alcohol. Stand at the prescription counter as person after person comes in to medicate their way out of loneliness. In this kind of world, love is not a pleasant extra. In this kind of world, love is a desperate requirement.

"Friends, we have to love each other." That includes every person here. John and Julie*, that includes the two of you. John and Julie*, you have to love each other. You have to love each other not just today, in the romantic luster of your wedding. You have to love each other tomorrow, next week, next month, and next year. You have to love each other when romance opens into reality and love is the only thing you have that can make your relationship continue to be the good thing for each other that it is today and you want it to be forever.

John and Julie*, you have to love each other. You have to work at loving each other. Sometimes that will be as easy as a wedding kiss. Sometimes that will be as difficult as having to forgive after you have been badly hurt. You have to work at loving each other when the world around you and inside you tries to dismantle and crumble your love to ruins. You have to continue to love each other. It is not a matter of wanting to. It is always a matter of needing to.

John and Julie*, there are a lot of things you are going to be doing in your life together. There is only one thing you *have* to do. John tells you what that is. You have to love each other. You have to love each other with as much care, commitment, faithfulness, and for as long as God loves you.

Amen.

Scriptural Index

Genesis
2:18	13
2:18-24	17, 19, 21, 24, 26, 28, 31, 33, 35, 37, 181
2:24	50
2-4	15

Numbers
6:24-26	40

Ruth
1:1-18	42
1:16-17	44, 46, 48

Psalm
23	52
100	86
128	50, 54, 56

Proverbs
21:21	58

Ecclesiastes
4:9-12	17, 60

Song of Solomon
4:10	84

Matthew
5:1-16	64
5:38-48	150
6:25-34	181
16:24-26	156
19:3-6	62
28:20	33

Mark
10:5-9	66

Luke
2:1-20	68
2:8-12	79
6:43-45	24
7:11-17	77
10:30-35	72
12:22-31	74
15:11-24	70

John
2:1-11	95
3:16	84
5:1-9	86
6:1-14	93
13:34	84, 99
13:35	84
15:1-17	97
15:9-13	99
15:9-16	90
15:9-17	86
15:12	88
15:12-16	28, 101
15:13	84
15:15	81
21:17	84

Romans		Philippians	
12	107	1:3-11	150
12:1-18	105	2:1-11	152, 154
12:1-21	103	2:5-8	156
12:2	140	4:4-9	130, 158, 161
12:9-18	121	4:8-9	107

1 Corinthians		Colossians	
12:31—13:8	113	3:12-14	163, 171
12:31—13:13	181	3:12-17	86, 168, 173
13	62, 110, 115, 117, 121, 124, 130, 132, 134, 136, 168	3:14	165
		2 Thessalonians	
		3:5	175
13:1-7	128		
13:1-8, 13	184	1 Timothy	
13:4-7	28, 37, 58	6:17-19	177
13:4-13	126		
13:13	84	James	
16:13-14	119	1:17-18	179
		3:2-12	181

2 Corinthians		1 Peter	
8:5	138	3:1-11	184

Galatians		1 John	
5:22-23a	140	3:18-24	113
		4:7-12	115, 191
Ephesians		4:7-19	186
4:2-3	58	4:7-21	188, 193, 195
5:21-33	28, 142, 144, 146, 148	4:14-21	126
		4:16	117
5:25	84	4:19	84

www.ingramcontent.com/pod-product-compliance
Lightning Source LLC
Chambersburg PA
CBHW061307110426
42742CB00012BA/2092